Fish of
Wisconsin

FIELD GUIDE

T0127076

by Dave Bosanko

Adventure Publications
Cambridge, Minnesota

ACKNOWLEDGEMENTS

Special thanks to the United States Fish and Wildlife Service, the Wisconsin Department of Natural Resources and the Minnesota Department of Natural Resources, particularly Roger Hugill.

Edited by Dan Johnson

Cover and book design by Jonathan Norberg

Photo/Illustration credits by artist and page number:

Cover illustrations: Muskellunge (main) and Bluegill (upper) by Joseph Tomelleri

Timothy Knepp/USFWS: 90, 92, 104, 106 **MN DNR:** 24, 25, 26 **MyFWC.com/fishing:** 29 **Duane Raver/USFWS:** 19, 27 (bottom), 30, 32, 34, 36, 38, 40, 42, 48, 50, 52, 54, 56, 66, 72, 74, (second inset), 80, 84, 94, 96 (top), 100, 124, 126, 128, 138, 140, 142, 144, 144, 146, 148, 150, 152, 156, 158, 162 **Joseph Tomelleri:** 27 (top), 28, 44 (both), 46, 58, 60, 62, 64, 68, 70, 74, 76, 78, 82 (both), 86, 94 (inset), 96 (bottom), 98 (main, inset 1), 102, 108, 110, 112 (main, insets), 114, 116, 118 (both), 120, 122, 130, 132, 134, 136, 154, 160, 164 **WI DNR:** 24 (lower right)

15 14 13 12 11 10 9 8

Fish of Wisconsin Field Guide
Copyright © 2007 by Dave Bosanko
Published by Adventure Publications
An imprint of AdventureKEEN
310 Garfield Street South
Cambridge, Minnesota 55008
(800) 678-7006
www.adventurepublications.net
Printed in China
ISBN 978-1-59193-194-2 (pbk.)

TABLE OF CONTENTS

HOW TO USE THIS BOOK

Your Fish of Wisconsin field guide is designed to make it easy to identify more than 70 species of the most common and important fish in Wisconsin, and learn fascinating facts about each species' range, natural history and more.

The fish are organized by families (such as Catfish, Perch, Pike and Sunfish), which are listed in alphabetical order. Within these families, individual species are also arranged alphabetically, in groups where necessary. For example, members of the Sunfish family are divided into Black Bass, Crappie and True Sunfish groups. For a detailed list of fish families and individual species, turn to the Table of Contents (pg. 3); the Index (pp. 172-175) provides a handy reference guide to fish by common name (such as Lake Trout) and other common terms for the species.

Fish Identification

Determining a fish's body shape is the first step to identifying it. Each fish family usually exhibits one or sometimes two basic outlines. Catfish have long, stout bodies with flattened heads, barbels or "whiskers" around the mouth, a relatively tall but narrow dorsal fin, and an adipose fin. There are two forms of sunfish: the flat, round, plate-like outline we see in Bluegills; and the torpedo or "fusiform" shape of bass.

In this field guide you can quickly identify your catch by first matching its general body shape to one of the fish family silhouettes listed in the Table of Contents (pp. 3-7). From there, turn to that family's section and use the illustrations and text descriptions to identify your fish. A Sample Page (pg. 30) is provided to explain how the information is presented in each two-page spread.

For some species, the illustration will be enough to identify your catch, but it is important to note that your fish may not look exactly like the picture. Fish frequently change colors. Males that are brightly colored during the spawning season may be dull silver at other times. Likewise, bass caught in muddy streams show much less pattern than those taken from clear lakes—and all fish lose some of their markings and color when they are removed from the water.

Most fish are similar in appearance to one or more other species—often, but not always, within the same family. For example, the Black Crappie is remarkably similar to its cousin the White Crappie. To accurately identify such look-alikes, check the inset illustrations and accompanying notes below the main illustration, under the "Similar Species" heading.

Throughout Fish of Wisconsin, we use basic biological and fisheries management terms that refer to physical characteristics or conditions of fish and their environment, such as dorsal fin or turbid water. For your convenience, these terms are defined in the Glossary (pp. 167-171), along with other handy fish-related terms and their definitions.

WISCONSIN FISH

Wisconsin is extremely blessed with aquatic resources. In addition to our extensive coastline on both Lake Superior and Lake Michigan, we have 14,949 inland lakes that spread over more than a million acres. Plus, there are 33,000 miles of streams and rivers in three major water-sheds. Of these streams, 1,500 are considered trout streams totaling nearly 8,700 miles. The large diversity of waters in Wisconsin provides an almost unlimited number of habitats for freshwater fish—and a profusion of opportunities to watch, study and pursue them.

There are approximately 157 species of fish in Wisconsin. Of these, thirty are the primary targets of fishermen. Another 40-plus species are of particular interest to those who spend time near the water, either because of their status as prized baitfish, unique characteristics or the likelihood you'll see them on forays to various freshwater habitats. Together, these species cover our major sport fish and provide an introduction to Wisconsin's major fish families.

FREQUENTLY ASKED QUESTIONS

What is a fish?

Fish are aquatic, cold-blooded animals with backbones, gills and fins.

Are all fish cold-blooded?

All freshwater fish are cold-blooded. Recently it has been discovered that some members of the saltwater tuna family are warm-blooded. Whales and dolphins are also warm-blooded, but they are mammals, not fish.

Do all fish have scales?

Most fish have scales that look like the ones found on the

common goldfish. A few, like gar, have scales that resemble armor plates. Some, such as catfish, have no scales at all.

How do fish breathe?

A fish takes in water through its mouth and forces it through its gills, where a system of fine membranes absorbs oxygen from the water, and releases carbon dioxide. Gills cannot pump air efficiently over these membranes, which quickly dry and stick together. Fish should never be out of the water longer than you can hold your breath.

Can fish breathe air?

Some species can; gars have a modified swim bladder that acts like a lung. Fish that can't breathe air may die when dissolved oxygen falls below critical levels, usually due to excessive rotting vegetation, and manure or chemical runoff.

How do fish swim?

Fish swim by contracting bands of muscles on alternate sides of their body, so the tail is whipped rapidly from side to side. Pectoral and pelvic fins are used mainly for stability when a fish hovers, but are sometimes used during rapid bursts of forward motion.

Do all fish look like fish?

Most do and are easily recognizable as fish. The eels and lampreys are fish, but they look like snakes. Sculpins look like little goblins with bat wings.

Where can you find fish?

Some fish species can be found in almost any body of

water, but not all fish are found everywhere. Each species is designed to exploit a particular habitat. One type of sculpin is found in clear, shallow creeks, while another lives in the depths of Lake Superior.

A species may move daily or seasonally within its home lake or stream. These movements may be horizontal, from one area to another, or vertically into deeper or shallower water.

Some are predictable seasonal migrations. In the spring, walleyes move to shallow, hard-bottom areas washed by winds or currents to spawn. Catfish frequently winter in deep holes of main rivers, and venture upstream, often into tributaries, during spring and summer.

Some movements are less predictable and are based on changing environmental conditions such as water temperature and clarity; the amount of dissolved oxygen; changes in predator or human activity; and food availability. Many fish have daily travel patterns; some predators suspend over deep water during the day, then move to structure or cover at peak feeding times.

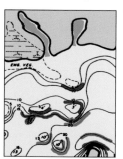

The graph at left, adapted from a hydrographic contour map, illustrates common locations for black crappies throughout the year in a typical section of a central Wisconsin lake.

Light green indicates early spring locations, when the crappies are feeding on minnows and other prey in shallow, fast-warming areas; **pink**

indicates hard-bottom spawning areas, often in bulrush beds; **dark green** highlights summertime areas; **brown** shows fall locations; and **light blue** indicates areas crappies are found from first-ice in December through March. Keep in mind that crappies (like many other species) often rise and fall in the water column in response to light levels and prey location. Depending on the food source and other factors, crappies will move closer to the surface at dawn, dusk and during the night, and drop close to bottom during the day.

Habitat such as aquatic vegetation also plays a major role in the location of many species throughout the year. For example, research has shown a strong correlation between healthy stands of vegetation and the summertime location of Blackchin Shiners—an important forage fish also considered an "indicator species" because it is sensitive to habitat degradation. Since these shiners favor the same habitat as juvenile game fish, any declines in the shiner population should be of great concern to anglers.

By studying a species' habitat, food and reproduction information in this book—and understanding how it interacts with other Wisconsin fish—it is possible to make an educated prediction of where to find it in any lake or river.

MAP RESOURCES

There are a number of sources of lake contour maps and aerial photos to help you pinpoint likely areas to look for fish. The Wisconsin DNR has maps for more than 1,300 lakes and rivers. It is in the process of digitizing them, and some are available for viewing on the website www.dnr.state.wi.us.

A variety of commercial mapping resources are available, including Sportsman's Connection: (888) 572-0182, www.sportsmansconnection.com; LakeMaster: (800) 540-5747, www.lakemaps.com; and Fishing Hot Spots: (800) 255-6277, www.fishinghotspots.com.

FISH NAMES

A Walleye is a Walleye in Wisconsin, where it's revered as a game fish. But in the northern parts of its range, Canadians call it a *jack* or *jackfish*. And in the eastern United States it is often grouped with other pike-shaped fish and called a *pickerel* or *walleyed pike*.

Because common names may vary regionally, and even change for different sizes of the same species, scientific names are used that are exactly the same around the world. Each species has only one correct scientific name that can be recognized anywhere, in any language. The Walleye is *Sander vitreus* from Madison to Moscow.

Scientific names are made up of Greek or Latin words that often describe the species. There are two parts to a scientific name, the generic or "genus," which is capitalized (*Sander*), and the specific name, which is not capitalized (*vitreus*). Scientific names are displayed in *italic* text. A species' genus represents a group of closely related fish. The Walleye and the Sauger are in the same genus, so they share the generic name *Sander*. But each have different specific names, *vitreus* for Walleye, *canadenses* for the Sauger. Thus the full scientific name for Walleye is *Sander vitreus* and *Sander canadenses* for the Sauger.

It is inappropriate to use the specific name without its accompanying generic name, as many species have the same specific name. Saugers and Canada geese share similar specific names. Without knowing the genus of your catch, it would be hard to know if it should be plucked or scaled.

FUN WITH FISH

There are many ways to enjoy Wisconsin's fish, from reading about them in this book to watching them in the wild. You can don a dive mask and jump in; wear polarized glasses to observe them from above the surface; or use an underwater camera (or sonar) to monitor fish behavior both during the open-water period and through the ice.

Hands-on activities are also popular. Most children and more than a few adults enjoy wading the shallows, catching small fish and other aquatic critters with a minnow net, bucket or their bare hands.

Another way to enjoy our wild fish is to collect a few and keep them in an aquarium. At press time in 2006, state law allowed residents to keep fish for aquarium use, under specific guidelines. Check the DNR website and fishing regulations for details.

RECREATIONAL FISHING

The fishing opportunities in Wisconsin are incredibly numerous and diverse. From trout and salmon in the Great Lakes to bluegills off the dock—and nearly everything in between—it's here. Small wonder, then, that 48 percent of adults statewide fish. As Mike Staggs, director of the DNR's Bureau of Fisheries puts it, "Fishing is a cornerstone of Wisconsin's culture and economy." Anglers outside our borders have also discovered this bounty, as Wisconsin ranks second in the U.S. in the number of days nonresidents spend fishing here.

Proceeds from license sales, along with special taxes anglers pay on fishing supplies and motorboat fuel, fund the majority of DNR fish management efforts, including fish surveys, the development of special regulations and stocking programs. The sport also has a huge impact on Wisconsin's economy, supporting in thousands of jobs in fishing, tourism and related industries.

LEARNING TO FISH

Learning to fish can be intimidating, especially if you have no one to teach you. Fortunately, help is available. One source is the DNR, which offers a wealth of information to help new anglers throughout the state. A variety of educational materials are available on the DNR website. In addition, a number of state and local fishing organizations, sportsmen's clubs and church groups hold events that teach people to fish.

SHARING THE SPORT

Most anglers in the United States say they fish because someone took the time to introduce them to the sport. As American lifestyles change, however, fewer people (especially youths) have access to a parent or grandparent as fishing mentors.

Recently, the Recreational Boating and Fishing Foundation, a non-profit organization, created a new program called Anglers' Legacy. The goal is to rally the country's estimated 7.5 million most-avid anglers to introduce at least one new person to fishing per year. For details, visit AnglersLegacy.org.

FISH MANAGEMENT

The DNR uses a variety of methods to manage Wisconsin's fish, including habitat protection and improvement; fish stocking; and gathering information through scientific surveys of fish populations, habitat and fishing activity.

The DNR also adjusts the fishing regulations to prevent overharvest. As anglers have become more proficient, fishing regulations have become more complex, particularly with the addition of special length, slot and bag limits. Management increasingly is on a lake-by-lake basis, as well, allowing fish managers to tailor the rules to enhance individual fisheries. Fortunately, fishing regulation handbooks are readily available wherever fishing licenses are sold, and on the DNR website. It is up to the responsible angler to help preserve fish populations. Please do your part and play by the rules.

CATCH-AND-RELEASE FISHING

The practices of selective harvest (keeping some fish to eat and releasing the rest) and total catch-and-release fishing allow anglers to enjoy the sport without harming the resource. Catch-and-release is especially important with certain species and sizes of fish, and in lakes or rivers where biologists are trying to improve the fishery by protecting large predators or breeding age, adult fish. The fishing regulations booklet, DNR website and your local DNR fisheries office are excellent sources of advice on which fish to keep and which to release.

In virtually all Wisconsin fisheries, trophy fish of every species are treasures too rare to be caught only once. Photographs and graphite replicas are ethical alternatives to killing a trophy fish simply for the purpose of displaying it.

FISH HANDLING TIPS

Catch-and-release is only truly successful if the fish survives the experience. Following are helpful tips to help reduce the chances of post-release mortality.

- Play and land fish quickly.

- Wet your hands before touching a fish, to avoid removing its protective slime coating.

- Handle the fish gently and keep it in the water as much as possible.

- Do not hold the fish by the eye sockets or gills. Hold it by the lower lip or under the gill plate—and support its belly.

- If a fish is deeply hooked, cut the line so at least an inch hangs outside the mouth. This helps the hook lie flush when the fish takes in food.

- Circle hooks may help reduce the number of deeply hooked fish.

- Avoid fishing in deep water unless you plan to keep your catch.

- Don't plan to release fish that have been on a stringer or in a livewell.

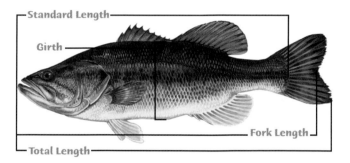

FISH MEASUREMENT

The length of a fish is measured in three ways: standard length; fork length; and total length. Standard length is used by ichthyologists (scientist that study fish). Fisheries biologists use fork length, and the general public uses total length. The first two are more accurate, because tails are often damaged or worn down in older fish. For anglers, total length is the most important, since it is used in determining the legality of the catch. (Note: Sturgeon are measured without pinching the tail. Use the top tip of the tail.) If you think your fish is a record catch, be sure to record both the total and fork lengths.

LENGTH-TO-WEIGHT RATIOS

It is possible to determine the approximate weight of a fish without weighing it on a scale, which can damage it or increase stress due to time out of the water. Using the formulas below (courtesy of the Wisconsin DNR), you can quickly determine the weight of popular game fish. Lengths are in inches; weight is in pounds.

Formulas

bass weight = (length x length x girth) / 1,200
pike weight = (length x length x length) / 3,500
sunfish weight = (length x length x length) / 1,200
trout weight = (length x girth x girth) / 800
walleye weight = (length x length x length) / 2,700

For example, let's say you catch a 16-inch Walleye. Using the Walleye formula above: (16 x 16 x 16) divided by 2,700 = 1.5 pounds. Your fish would weigh approximately 1.5 pounds.

RECORD FISH

Most states maintain lists of state-record fish. World records are kept by the National Fresh Water Fishing Hall of Fame and the International Game Fish Association. Each organization has its own standards and procedures for recognizing record fish. The North American records used in this book are those recorded by the National Fresh Water Fishing Hall of Fame. If you think you have caught a state or world record and want to register it follow these steps:

- Contact the organization you wish to record your fish with to acquire the correct forms and procedures.
- Measure the total and fork length of your fish. Measure the girth of your fish at its largest point.
- Weigh your fish on a state-certified scale (most commercial scales).
- Have all measurements and weights witnessed and the scale certification number recorded.
- Have your fish identified at a DNR fisheries office.
- Take a clear color picture of you holding your fish.
- Keep your fish whole, either fresh or frozen.

Helpful contacts include:

Wisconsin Department of Natural Resources
www.dnr.wi.gov; (608) 266-2621

National Fresh Water Fishing Hall of Fame
www.Freshwater-Fishing.org; (715) 634-4440

International Game Fish Association
www.igfa.org; (954) 927-2628

WISCONSIN STATE RECORD FISH

SPECIES	WEIGHT (LBS.-OZ.)	WHERE CAUGHT	YEAR
Bass, Largemouth	11-3	Lake Ripley	1940
Bass, Rock	2-15	Shadow Lake	1990
Bass, Smallmouth	9-1	Indian Lake	1950
Bass, Hybrid Striped	13-14.2	Lake Columbia	2002
Bass, Striped	1-9.8	Fox River	1996
Bass, White	4-6	Okauchee Lake	1977
Bass, Yellow	2-12	Lake Waubesa	2013
Bluegill	2-9.8	Green Bay	1995
Bowfin	13-1	Willow Flowage	1980
Buffalo, Bigmouth	76-8	Pentenwell Flowage	2013
Buffalo, Smallmouth	20-0	Milwaukee River	1999
Bullhead, Black	5-8	Big Falls Flowage	1989
Bullhead, Brown	4-2	Little Green Lake	2006
Bullhead, Yellow	3-5	Nelson Lake	1983
Burbot	18-2	Lake Superior	2002
Carp, Common	57-2	Lake Wisconsin	1966
Carpsucker, Quillback	9-15.8	Wolf River	2016
Catfish, Channel	44	Wisconsin River	1962
Catfish, Flathead	74-5	Mississippi River	2001
Chub, Creek	0-9.6	Unnamed Lake	2011
Cisco	4-10.5	Big Green Lake	1969
Crappie, Black	4-8	Gile Flowage	1967
Crappie, White	3-13.1	Cranberry Marsh	2003
Drum, Freshwater	35-4	Mississippi River	1992
Eel, American	3-6	Lake Superior	1997
Gar, Longnose	21-4	Wisconsin River	1990
Gar, Shortnose	4-5.8	Mississippi River	2015
Goby, Round	0-5.3	Lake Michigan	2008
Mooneye	2-6.6	Mississippi River	2014
Muskellunge	69-11	Chippewa Flowage	1949
Muskellunge, Tiger	51-3	Lac Vieux Desert	1919
Perch, White	1-5.4	Green Bay	2005
Perch, Yellow	3-4	Lake Winnebago	1954

SPECIES	WEIGHT (LBS.-OZ.)	WHERE CAUGHT	YEAR
Pike, Northern	38-0	Lake Puckaway	1952
Pumpkinseed	1-2	Big Round Lake	2003
Redhorse, Silver	11-7	Plum Creek	1985
Salmon, Atlantic	23-15	Lake Michigan	1980
Salmon, Chinook (King)	44-15	Lake Michigan	1994
Salmon, Coho	26-1.9	Lake Michigan	1999
Salmon, Kokanee	2-8.2	Upper Bass Lake	2007
Salmon, Pink	6-1.9	Lake Michigan	1999
Salmon, Pinook	9-1.6	Lake Michigan	2016
Sauger	6-6.7	Mississippi River	2009
Splake	17-14.5	Green Bay	2002
Sturgeon, Lake	170-10	Yellow Lake	1979
Sturgeon, Shovelnose	7-5.4	Mississippi River	1998
Sucker, Northern Hog.	1-13	Fox River	2004
Sucker, White	6-2	Miller Flowage	1997
Sunfish, Green	1-9	Wind Lake	1967
Trout, Brook (inland)	9-15	Prairie River	1944
Trout, Brook (outlying)	10-1	Lake Michigan	1999
Trout, Brown (inland)	18-6	Lake Geneva	1984
Trout, Brown (outlying)	41-8	Lake Michigan	2010
Trout, Lake (inland)	35-4	Big Green Lake	1957
Trout, Lake (outlying)	47-0	Lake Superior	1946
Trout, Rainbow (inland)	12-3	Elbow Lake	2006
Trout, Rainbow (outlying)	27-2	Lake Michigan	1997
Trout, Tiger	20-13	Lake Michigan	1978
Walleye	18-0	High Lake	1933
Warmouth	1-1	Eagle Lake	2001
Whitefish, Lake	12-6.4	Lake Michigan	2013

FISH CONSUMPTION ADVISORIES

Most fish are safe to eat and a healthy source of low-fat protein. But because most of the world's surface water contains some industrial contaminants—and Wisconsin's lakes and rivers are no exception—any store-bought or sport-caught fish could contain mercury, PCBs or other contaminants.

The Wisconsin DNR has detailed information on eating fish, including advisories on fish consumption for sport-caught species. For details, call the Bureau of Fisheries Management and Habitat Protection, (608) 267-7498, or visit www.dnr.wi.gov.

FISH DISEASES

Like other living creatures, fish are susceptible to various parasites, infections and diseases. Fish are especially vulnerable when stressed by environmental factors such as rapid warming of the water temperature, and after traumatic events, including being wounded by a predator or improperly handled by an angler. Conditions found in Wisconsin include:

  Neascus (Black spot disease): Caused by tiny parasites that produce black spots resembling black pepper sprinkled on fins or fillets. Fish that inhabit shallow water are most affected. The condition is very common throughout the state, but experts say the fish are edible if well cooked.

Heterosporis: Predominantly seen in Yellow Perch, the disease has also been found in Walleyes, Northern Pike, Trout-perch, Burbot, Pumpkinseed, Sculpin and Rock Bass. Heterosporis is a microscopic parasite that infects muscle tissue of fish by producing millions of spores, which destroy muscle tissue. Infected area looks like white or "opaque areas" in the uncooked fish fillet. Little is known about the life cycle, but it is believed the disease may be spread by infected Fathead Minnows sold as bait. There is no evidence heterosporis can infect people. It is thought, but not proven; that thoroughly cooking infected fish will destroy spores.

Myofibrogranuloma: Only recorded in walleyes, it is caused by a virus and not considered infectious. Environmental conditions and genetics may play a role in its development. An affected fish looks normal externally, but areas of the fillet appear semi-translucent or yellow brown, with knotted muscle fibers.

The tissue has a dry appearance and may appear granular with mineral deposits. Anglers are advised not to eat fish with this condition.

Dermal Sarcoma: Grape-like tumors only seen in Walleyes. Condition produces warty growths on the fish's skin and fins. Growths are usually gray-white or pinkish in color. Infections occur any time but are more common during the spawn, when virus is spread through physical contact. Not known to affect humans; always cook fish thoroughly.

 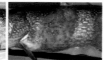 **Lymphosarcoma:** A cauliflower-like tumor on the skin, it is most likely caused by a virus and transmitted by physical contact. Affects Muskies and Northern Pike; tumors range up to several inches in size, depending on water temperature. It is more prominent at cooler water temperatures, and the tumor may spread to the fish's inner organs. Consumption of affected fish not advised.

INVASIVE SPECIES

Exotic, invasive aquatic species are a threat to native plants, fish and animals—as well as water-based recreation, particularly fishing. The invaders come in many forms, but the results are consistently negative. Eurasian Watermilfoil produces thick surface mats that crowd out native plants; the Round Goby displaces native fish; Zebra Mussels crowd out native mussels and disrupt entire lake ecosystems. And these are just a few of the invaders.

There are a number of things you can do to slow the spread of exotic species across Wisconsin. In general, cleaning your boat and emptying your livewell and minnow pail on dry land will go a long way toward slowing the spread of invasive species. Current information on specific invasive species is available on the DNR website.

FISH ANATOMY

To identify fish, you will need to know a few basic terms that apply to fins and their locations.

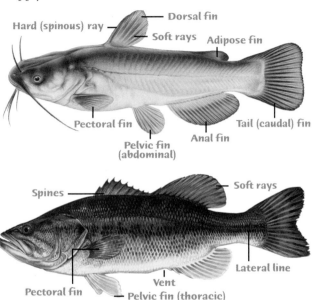

Fins are made up of bony structures that support a membrane. There are three kinds of bony structures in fins. **Soft rays** are fixable fin supports and are often branched. **Spines** are stiff, often sharp supports that are not jointed. **Hard rays** are stiff, pointed, barbed structures that can be raised or lowered. Catfish are famous for their hard rays, which are often mistakenly called spines. Sunfish have soft rays associated with spines to form a prominent dorsal fin.

Fins are named by their position on the fish. The **dorsal fin** is on top along the midline. A few species have another fin on their back, called an **adipose fin**. This is small, fleshy protuberance located between the dorsal fin and the tail is distinctive of trout and catfish. **Pectoral fins** are found on each side of the fish near the gills. The **anal fin** is located along the midline, on the fish's bottom or ventral side. There is also a paired set of fins on the bottom of the fish, called the **pelvic fins**. Pelvic fins can be in the **thoracic position** (just below the pectoral fins) or farther back on the stomach, in the **abdominal position**. The tail is known as the **caudal fin**.

Other important parts of fish anatomy and their functions include the following:

Eyes—A fish's eyes can detect color. Their eyes are rounder than those of mammals because of the refractive index of water; focus is achieved by moving the lens in and out, not distorting it as in mammals. Fish have varying levels of sight. Walleyes have great low-light vision; bluegills have acute daytime vision but can't see well in low light; and catfish have extremely poor eyesight, day or night.

Nostrils—A pair of nostrils, or *nares*, are used to detect odors in the water. Eels and catfishes have particularly well-developed senses of smell.

Mouth—The shape of the mouth is a clue to what the fish eats. The larger the food it consumes, the larger the mouth.

Teeth—Not all fish have teeth, but those that do have mouthgear designed to help them feed. Walleyes, northern pike and muskies have sharp **canine** teeth for grabbing and holding prey. Minnows have *pharyngeal* teeth—located in the throat—for grinding. Catfish have *cardiform* teeth, which feel like a rough patch in the front of the mouth. Bass have tiny patches of **vomerine** teeth in the roof of their mouth.

Swim Bladder—Almost all fish have a swim bladder, a balloon-like organ that helps the fish regulate its buoyancy.

Lateral Line—This sensory organ helps the fish detect movement in the water (to help avoid predators or capture prey) as well as water currents and pressure changes. It consists of fluid-filled sacs with hair-like sensors, which are open to the water through a row of pores in their skin along each side—creating a visible line along the fish's side.

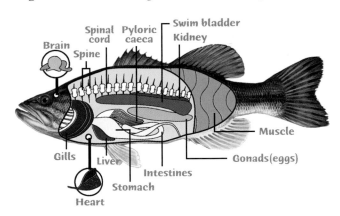

Description: brief summary of physical characteristics to help you identify the fish, such as coloration and markings, body shape, fin size and placement

Similar Species: Lists other fish that look similar and the pages on which they can be found. Also includes detailed inset drawings (below) highlighting physical traits such as markings, mouth size or shape and fin characteristics to help you distinguish this fish from similar species

Walleye	**Sauger**		**Walleye**	**Sauger**

white spot on bottom of tail	no white spot on tail		spiny dorsal fin lacks spots, has large dark spot on rear base	spiny dorsal fin is spotted, lacks dark blotch on rear base

COMMON NAME
Scientific Name

Other Names: common terms or nicknames you may hear to describe this species

Habitat: environment where the fish is found (such as streams, rivers, small or large lakes, fast-flowing or still water, in or around vegetation, near shore, in clear water)

Range: geographic distribution, starting with the fish's overall range, followed by state-specific information

Food: what the fish eats most of the time (such as crustaceans, insects, fish, plankton)

Reproduction: timing of and behavior during the spawning period (dates and water temperatures, migration information, preferred spawning habitat, type of nest if applicable, colonial or solitary nester, parental care for eggs or fry)

Average Size: average length or range of length, average weight or range of weight

Records: State—the state record for this species, location and year; North American—the North American record for this species, location and year (from the National Fresh Water Fishing Hall of Fame)

Notes: Interesting natural history information. This can be unique behaviors, remarkable features, sporting and table quality, or details on migrations, seasonal patterns or population trends.

Description: long, stout body; rounded tail; continuous dorsal fin; bony plates covering head; brownish green back and sides with white belly; males have large "eye" spot at the base of tail

Similar Species: Burbot (pg. 46), American Eel (pg. 50), Sea Lamprey (pg. 62)

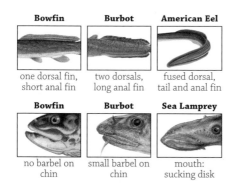

Bowfin	**Burbot**	**American Eel**
one dorsal fin, short anal fin	two dorsals, long anal fin	fused dorsal, tail and anal fin

Bowfin	**Burbot**	**Sea Lamprey**
no barbel on chin	small barbel on chin	mouth: sucking disk

BOWFIN
Amia calva

Other Names: dogfish, grindle, mudfish, cypress trout, lake lawyer, beaverfish

Habitat: deep waters associated with weedbeds in warm water lakes and rivers; feeds in shallow weeds

Range: Mississippi River drainage east through St. Lawrence drainage, south from Texas to Florida; in Wisconsin, common in the Mississippi River drainage, the Fox-Wolf River system and lower Green Bay; known only from the St. Louis and Middle rivers in the Lake Superior drainage

Food: fish, crayfish

Reproduction: when water warms past 61 degrees in spring, male removes vegetation on sand or gravel bottom; one or more females deposit up to 5,000 eggs in nest; male guards until young reach about 4 inches in length

Average Size: 12 to 24 inches, 2 to 5 pounds

Records: State—13 pounds, 1 ounce; Willow Flowage, Oneida County, 1980; North American—21 pounds, 8 ounces; Forest Lake, South Carolina, 1980

Notes: Though the Bowfin's gluttony has been exaggerated, it is still a voracious predator that prowls shallow weedbeds, preying on anything that moves. Once thought harmful to game fish, it is now considered an asset in controlling rough fish and stunted game fish populations. The Bowfin is an air breather that can survive in oxygen-depleted waters, as well as muddy cavities in drying lakes.

33

Description: black to olive-green back; sides yellowish green; belly creamy to yellow; light bar on base of tail; barbels (dark at base) around mouth; adipose fin; scaleless skin; rounded tail

Similar Species: Brown Bullhead (pg. 36), Yellow Bullhead (pg. 38), Madtom/Stonecat (pg. 44), Flathead Catfish (pg. 42)

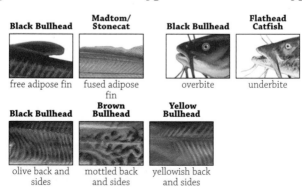

Black Bullhead	**Madtom/ Stonecat**	**Black Bullhead**	**Flathead Catfish**
free adipose fin	fused adipose fin	overbite	underbite

Black Bullhead	**Brown Bullhead**	**Yellow Bullhead**
olive back and sides	mottled back and sides	yellowish back and sides

BLACK BULLHEAD

Ameiurus melas

Other Names: common bullhead, horned pout

Habitat: shallow, slow-moving streams and backwaters; lakes and ponds; tolerates extremely turbid (cloudy) conditions

Range: southern Canada through the Great Lakes and the Mississippi River watershed into Mexico and the Southwest; common throughout Wisconsin

Food: a scavenging opportunist, feeds mostly on animal material (live or dead) but will eat plant matter

Reproduction: spawns from late April to early June; builds nest in shallow water with a muddy bottom; both sexes guard nest and eggs; male guards young to 1 inch in size

Average Size: 8 to 10 inches, 4 ounces to 1 pound

Records: State—5 pounds, 8 ounces; Big Falls Flowage, Rusk County, 1989; North American—8 pounds, 15 ounces; Sturgis Pond, Michigan, 1987

Notes: The Black Bullhead is the smallest and most abundant of the three bullhead species found in Wisconsin. It is also the one most tolerant of silt, pollution and low oxygen levels. Bullheads are common and easily caught in Wisconsin but get little respect. Black bullheads are prolific and can quickly overpopulate a pond, resulting in stunted fish.

Description: yellowish brown upper body, with mottling on back and sides; barbels around mouth; adipose fin; scaleless skin; rounded tail; well-defined barbs on the pectoral spines

Similar Species: Black Bullhead (pg. 34), Yellow Bullhead (pg. 38), Madtom/Stonecat (pg. 44), Flathead Catfish (pg. 42)

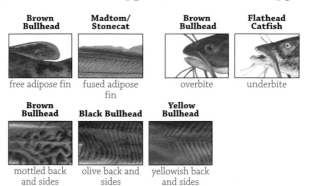

Brown Bullhead	Madtom/ Stonecat	Brown Bullhead	Flathead Catfish
free adipose fin	fused adipose fin	overbite	underbite

Brown Bullhead	Black Bullhead	Yellow Bullhead
mottled back and sides	olive back and sides	yellowish back and sides

BROWN BULLHEAD

Ameiurus nebulosus

Other Names: marbled or speckled bullhead, red cat

Habitat: warm, weedy lakes and sluggish streams

Range: southern Canada through the Great Lakes down the eastern states to Florida; introduced in the West; in Wisconsin, present in Lake Superior, Michigan and Mississippi drainages, most common in the Rock, Fox-Wolf and Chippewa river systems

Food: a scavenging opportunist; feeds mostly on insects, fish, fish eggs, snails and leeches but will eat plant matter

Reproduction: in early summer females and males build nest in shallow water with a sand or rocky bottom, often in cover offering shade; both sexes guard eggs and young

Average Size: 8 to 10 inches, 4 ounces to 2 pounds

State Record: State—4 pounds, 2 ounces, Little Green Lake, Little Green County, 2006; North American—6 pounds, 2 ounces, Pearl River, Mississippi, 1991

Notes: The Brown Bullhead is very abundant in Mississippi backwaters, but also inhabits northern Walleye lakes. It can tolerate very turbid (cloudy) water but prefers clean, weedy lakes with soft bottoms. Young bullheads are black, and in early summer are often seen swimming in a tight, swarming ball. An adult fish may be seen guarding this ball of fry. Not highly pursued by anglers, though its reddish meat is tasty and fine table fare.

Description: olive head and back; yellowish-green sides; white belly; barbels on lower jaw are pale green to white; scaleless skin, adipose fin, rounded tail

Similar Species: Brown Bullhead (pg. 36), Black Bullhead (pg. 34), Madtom/Stonecat (pg. 44), Flathead Catfish (pg. 42)

Yellow Bullhead	Madtom/ Stonecat	Yellow Bullhead	Flathead Catfish
free adipose fin	fused adipose fin	overbite	underbite

Yellow Bullhead	Brown Bullhead	Black Bullhead
yellowish back and sides	mottled back and sides	olive back and sides

YELLOW BULLHEAD

Ameiurus natalis

Other Names: white-whiskered bullhead, yellow cat

Habitat: warm, weedy lakes and sluggish streams

Range: southern Great Lakes through the eastern half of the U.S. to the Gulf and into Mexico; introduced in the West; common in most of Wisconsin except the Mississippi River basin in the southwest third of the state

Food: a scavenging opportunist, feeds on insects, crayfish, snails, small fish and plant material

Reproduction: in late spring to early summer, males and females build nest in shallow water with some vegetation and a soft bottom; both sexes guard eggs and young

Average Size: 8 to 10 inches, 1 to 2 pounds

Records: State—3 pounds, 5 ounces; Nelson Lake, Sawyer County, 1983; North American—4 pounds, 15 ounces; Ogeechee River, Georgia, 2003

Notes: The Yellow Bullhead is common in Wisconsin's inland lakes. Its cream-colored flesh has excellent flavor, but may become soft in summer. Bullheads feed by "taste," locating their food by following chemical trails through the water. This ability can be greatly diminished in polluted water, impairing their ability to find food. The Yellow Bullhead is less likely than other bullheads to overpopulate a lake and become stunted.

Description: gray to silver back and sides; white belly; black spots on sides; large fish lack spots and appear dark olive or slate; forked tail; adipose fin; long barbels around mouth

Similar Species: Blue Catfish, Flathead Catfish (pg. 42), Bullheads (pp. 34-39)

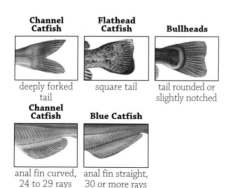

Channel Catfish	Flathead Catfish	Bullheads
deeply forked tail	square tail	tail rounded or slightly notched

Channel Catfish	Blue Catfish
anal fin curved, 24 to 29 rays	anal fin straight, 30 or more rays

CHANNEL CATFISH

Ictalurus punctatus

Other Names: spotted, speckled or silver catfish

Habitat: prefers clean, fast-moving streams with deep pools; stocked in many lakes; can tolerate turbid (cloudy) water

Range: southern Canada through the Midwest into Mexico and Florida; introduced through much of the U.S.; in Wisconsin, widely distributed in the southern two-thirds of state in both the Mississippi and Lake Michigan drainage basins; in the north, Channel Catfish are known only from the St. Louis River drainage

Food: insects, crustaceans, fish, some plant debris

Reproduction: in early summer male builds nest in dark, sheltered area such as an undercut bank or under logs; female deposits gelatinous egg mass; male guards eggs and young until the nest is deserted

Average Size: 12 to 20 inches, 3 to 4 pounds

Records: State—44 pounds; Wisconsin River, Columbia County, 1962; North American—58 pounds, Santee Cooper Reservoir, South Carolina, 1964

Notes: Channel Catfish rank high among sport fish in southeastern Wisconsin near the Mississippi River, but are not as highly regarded in the rest of the state. Considered by many to be fine table fare, they are prized by commercial fishermen along the Mississippi. Like other catfish, channels will feed both night and day; serious cat-fishermen often pursue them at night. Very similar in appearance to the southern Blue Catfish, which is rare in Wisconsin waters.

41

Description: color variable, usually mottled yellow or brown; belly cream to yellow; adipose fin; chin barbels; lacks scales; head broad and flattened; tail squared; pronounced underbite

Similar Species: Channel Catfish (pg. 40), Tadpole Madtom (pg. 44), Bullheads (pp. 34-39)

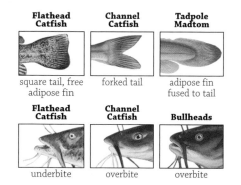

Flathead Catfish	**Channel Catfish**	**Tadpole Madtom**
square tail, free adipose fin	forked tail	adipose fin fused to tail

Flathead Catfish	**Channel Catfish**	**Bullheads**
underbite	overbite	overbite

FLATHEAD CATFISH

Pylodictis olivaris

Other Names: shovel-nose, shovelhead, yellow cat, mud cat, pied cat, Mississippi cat

Habitat: deep pools of large rivers and impoundments

Range: the Mississippi River watershed and into Mexico; large rivers in the Southwest; in Wisconsin, primarily in the Mississippi River and its large tributaries, and the upper Fox and lower Wolf rivers in the Lake Michigan drainage

Food: fish, crayfish

Reproduction: spawns when water is 72 to 80 degrees; male builds and defends nest in hollow log, undercut bank or other secluded area; female may lay more than 30,000 eggs, depending on her size and condition

Average Size: 20 to 30 inches, 10 to 20 pounds

Records: State—74 pounds, 5.1 ounces; Mississippi River, Vernon County, 2001; North American—123 pounds; Elk River Reservoir, Kansas, 1998

Notes: The Flathead Catfish is a large, typically solitary predator that inhabits Wisconsin's major river systems. It often relates to logjams and deep pools. Feeds aggressively on live fish; rarely eats decaying animal matter. Has been introduced into some lakes to control stunted panfish. A strong fighter with firm, white flesh. The St. Croix River below Taylors Falls is well known for large flatheads.

STONECAT

TADPOLE MADTOM

Description: Tadpole Madtom—dark olive to brown; dark line on side; large, fleshy head; Stonecat—similar but lacks dark lateral stripe, and has protruding upper jaw; both species have adipose fin continuous with tail

Similar Species: Bullheads (pp. 34-39), Catfish (pp. 40-43)

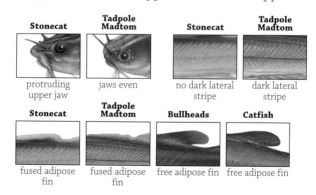

Stonecat	Tadpole Madtom	Stonecat	Tadpole Madtom
protruding upper jaw	jaws even	no dark lateral stripe	dark lateral stripe

Stonecat	Tadpole Madtom	Bullheads	Catfish
fused adipose fin	fused adipose fin	free adipose fin	free adipose fin

STONECAT *Noturus flavus*
TADPOLE MADTOM *Noturus gyrinus*

Ictaluridae

Other Name: willow cat

Habitat: weedy water near shore, under rocks in stream riffles

Range: eastern U.S.; Stonecats are found in all three drainage basins in Wisconsin; Tadpole Madtoms are also found statewide, including sheltered bays of Lake Superior

Food: small invertebrates, algae and other plant matter

Reproduction: spawn in late spring; not nest builders; female lays eggs under objects such as roots, rocks, logs or in abandoned crayfish burrows; nest guarded by one parent

Average Size: Tadpole Madtom—3 to 4 inches; Stonecat—4 to 6 inches

Records: none

Notes: Small, secretive fish most active at night. Both species have venom glands at the base of the dorsal and pectoral fins. Though not lethal, the venom produces a painful burning sensation, reputed to bring even the hardiest anglers to their knees, if only for a short time. Stonecats, and to a lesser degree Tadpole Madtoms, are common bait-fish in southern Wisconsin. They are favored by many veteran river walleye anglers, who believe the tough little baitfish are superior to minnows and chubs. Indeed, more than a few high-stakes walleye tournaments have been won by fishermen using "willow cats." Reportedly, damaging the "slime" coating (by rolling them in sand to make handling easier) will reduce their effectiveness as bait.

Description: eel-like body; mottled brown with creamy chin and belly; small barbel at each nostril opening, longer barbel on chin; rear part of dorsal similar in shape and just above anal fin

Similar Species: Bowfin (pg. 32), American Eel (pg. 50), Sea Lamprey (pg. 62)

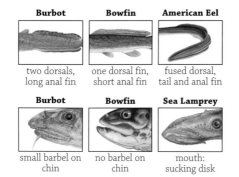

Burbot	Bowfin	American Eel
two dorsals, long anal fin	one dorsal fin, short anal fin	fused dorsal, tail and anal fin

Burbot	Bowfin	Sea Lamprey
small barbel on chin	no barbel on chin	mouth: sucking disk

BURBOT
Lota lota

Other Names: lawyer, eelpout, ling, cusk

Habitat: deep, cold, clear lakes and streams of the north

Range: northern North America into Siberia and across northern Europe; found throughout Wisconsin, common in the St. Croix, Chippewa-Red, Cedar, Wisconsin, Rock and Wolf-Fox river drainages

Food: a voracious predator; primarily feeds on small fish but will attempt to eat virtually anything, including fish eggs, clams and crayfish

Reproduction: pairs to large groups spawn together in mid- to late winter, under the ice, over sand or gravel bottoms, usually in less than 15 feet of water; after spawning, thrashing adults scatter fertilized eggs; no nest is built and there is no parental care

Average Size: 20 inches, 2 to 8 pounds

Records: State—18 pounds, 2 ounces; Lake Superior, Bayfield County, 2002; North American—22 pounds, 8 ounces; Little Athapapuskow Lake, Manitoba, 1994

Notes: A freshwater member of the cod family, the Burbot is a coldwater fish, seldom found in fisheries where the water temperature routinely exceeds 69 degrees. It is popular with ice fishermen in some western states and Scandinavia but is not highly regarded in Wisconsin despite its firm, white, good-tasting flesh.

Description: humped back, dorsal fin extends from hump to near tail; back is gray with purple or bronze reflections, silver sides, white underbelly; only Wisconsin fish with lateral line running from head through the tail

Similar Species: White Bass (pg. 158)

Freshwater Drum	**White Bass**	**Freshwater Drum**	**White Bass**
triangular tail	forked tail	downturned mouth	upturned mouth

FRESHWATER DRUM

Aplodinotus grunniens

Other Names: sheepshead, croaker, thunderpumper, grinder, bubbler (commercially marketed as white perch)

Habitat: slow- to moderate-current areas of rivers and streams; shallow lakes, often with mud or sand bottoms; prefers turbid (cloudy) water

Range: Canada south through Midwest into eastern Mexico to Guatemala; in Wisconsin, common in the Mississippi River drainage, Green Bay and its major tributaries

Food: small fish, insects, crayfish, clams, Zebra Mussels

Reproduction: in May and June after water temperature reaches about 66 degrees, schools of drum randomly lay eggs in open water near surface, over sand or gravel; no nest or parental care

Average Size: 10 to 14 inches, 2 to 5 pounds

Records: State—35 pounds, 4 ounces; Mississippi River, Crawford County, 1992; North American—54 pounds, 8 ounces; Nickajack Lake, Tennessee, 1972

Notes: Drum are named for the grunting or rumbling noise made by males, primarily to attract females; the sound is produced by specialized muscles rubbed along the swim bladder. Lake Winnebago holds a large drum population and in some years there has been a huge commercial harvest. Flaky white flesh is tasty but easily dries out when cooked due to its low oil content. The skull contains two large L-shaped ear stones called otoliths, once used for jewelry by Native Americans.

Description: long, snake-like body with large mouth, pectoral fins, gill slits and continuous dorsal, tail and anal fin; dark brown on top with yellow sides and white belly

Similar Species: Sea Lamprey (pg. 62), Bowfin (pg. 32), Burbot (pg. 46)

American Eel	**Bowfin**	**Burbot**
fused dorsal, tail and anal fin	one dorsal fin, short anal fin	two dorsals, long anal fin

American Eel	**Sea Lamprey**
mouth: jaws	mouth: sucking disk

50

AMERICAN EEL
Anguillidae

Anguilla rostrata

Other Names: common, Boston, Atlantic or freshwater eel

Habitat: soft bottoms of medium to large streams

Range: Atlantic Ocean, eastern and central North America, eastern Central America; in Wisconsin, the Mississippi River drainage system; less common in the Great Lakes drainages

Food: insects, crayfish and small fish

Reproduction: Wisconsin's only "catadromous" species, it spends most of its life in freshwater and spawns in the mid-North Atlantic Ocean in the Sargasso Sea; female may lay up to 20 million eggs; adults die after spawning

Average Size: 24 to 36 inches

Records: State—3 pounds, 6 ounces; Lake Superior, Ashland County, 1997; North American—8 pounds, 8 ounces; Cliff Pond, Massachusetts, 1992

Notes: Leaf-shaped larval eels drift with ocean currents for about a year. When they reach river mouths of North and Central America, they morph into small eels (elvers). Males remain in estuaries; females migrate upstream. At maturity (up to 20 years of age) adults return to Sargasso Sea. Not a popular food fish in Wisconsin but commercially fished along the East Coast. Most active at night.

Description: long, cylindrical profile; single dorsal fin located above anal fin; body is encased in hard, plate-like scales; snout twice as long as head; needle-sharp teeth on both jaws; olive to brown with dark spots along sides

Similar Species: Shortnose Gar (pg. 54)

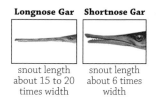

Longnose Gar	**Shortnose Gar**
snout length about 15 to 20 times width	snout length about 6 times width

LONGNOSE GAR

Lepisosteidae

Lepisosteus osseus

Other Names: gar, garfish

Habitat: floodplain lakes and backwaters of large rivers

Range: central U.S. through the Mississippi drainage south into Mexico; in Wisconsin, common in the Mississippi River and Lake Michigan drainages; rare in the Lake Superior drainage

Food: minnows and small fish

Reproduction: large, green eggs are laid in weedy shallows of lakes or tributaries when water temperatures reach the high 60s; using a small disk on the snout, a newly hatched gar attaches itself to a nearby plant, rock or wood until its mouth and digestive tract forms enough to begin feeding

Average Size: 24 to 36 inches, 2 to 5 pounds

Records: State—21 pounds, 4 ounces; Wisconsin River, Washington County, 1990; North American—50 pounds, 5 ounces; Trinity River, Texas, 1954

Notes: The Longnose Gar can breathe air at the surface, thanks to a modified swim bladder; this allows it to survive in hot shallows lacking enough oxygen for most other fish. Prefers warm, deep water but will school near the surface. An efficient predator that helps control rough fish populations, it stalks small fish, then makes a quick, sideways slash to capture them. May grow to lengths of five feet. A very hardy fish, it is well suited to our increasingly silty streams—and is a valuable asset in the control of rough fish populations.

53

Description: long, cylindrical body with toothy jaws and hard, diamond-shaped scales; snout is 1.3 times the length of head; back and sides olive to slate green; white belly; spots on rear third of the body

Similar Species: Longnose Gar (pg. 52)

Shortnose Gar   **Longnose Gar**

snout length   snout length
about 6 times   about 15 to 20
     width   times width

SHORTNOSE GAR

Lepisosteus platostomus

Other Names: stubnose, broadnose or shortbilled gar

Habitat: open water of warm, slow-moving streams, backwaters and shallow oxbow lakes

Range: Mississippi River drainage from the southern Great Lakes to Mexico; in Wisconsin, lakes and streams in the southern third of state, common in Lake St. Croix

Food: minnows, small fish, crayfish

Reproduction: spawns from May through June in quiet backwaters when water temperatures reach the mid-60s; yellowish green eggs are poisonous to mammals

Average Size: 12 to 24 inches, 1 to 3 pounds

Records: State—2 pounds, 12 ounces, Mississippi River, Grant County, 1999; North American—6 pounds, 6 ounces, Kentucky Lake, Tennessee, 2001

Notes: The Shortnose Gar is not as common in Wisconsin as the Longnose Gar. It prefers somewhat more active water and can tolerate higher turbidity (cloudiness) than other gar species. Like the Longnose, it can "gulp" air at the surface. An ambush predator, it is often seen floating near brush piles at the current's edge or along windswept shorelines. Flesh is considered poor table fare, though some anglers target gar using lures with nylon strands instead of hooks, which tangle in its teeth.

Description: silvery with blue to blue-green metallic shine on back with silver sides and white belly; faint dark stripes along sides; dark spot behind the gill, directly above the pectoral fin; large mouth with protruding lower jaw

Similar Species: Gizzard Shad (pg. 58), Goldeye/Mooneye (pp. 76-79)

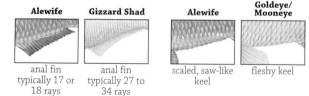

Alewife	**Gizzard Shad**	**Alewife**	**Goldeye/ Mooneye**
anal fin typically 17 or 18 rays	anal fin typically 27 to 34 rays	scaled, saw-like keel	fleshy keel

ALEWIFE

Alosa pseudoharengus

Clupeidae

Other Names: ellwife, sawbelly, shad or golden shad, big-eyed herring, river herring

Habitat: open water of the Great Lakes and a few inland lakes

Range: Atlantic Ocean from Labrador to Florida; in Wisconsin, St. Lawrence River drainage and the Great Lakes

Food: zooplankton, filamentous algae

Reproduction: in the Great Lakes, spawning takes place in open water of bays and along protected shorelines during early summer

Average Size: 4 to 8 inches

Records: none

Notes: This Atlantic herring reached the upper Great Lakes in 1931, Lake Huron in 1933, Lake Michigan in 1949 and Lake Superior in 1953. With the depletion of large predators by the Sea Lamprey the Alewife population had exploded in Lakes Michigan and Huron by the late 1950s to early 1960s. There is a much smaller population of Alewives in Lake Superior. Not well adapted to freshwater lakes the Alewife is subject to frequent large summerkills. The Alewife is the main forage for the salmon and Lake Trout in the Great Lakes and is used commercially for animal food.

Description: deep body; silvery blue back with white sides and belly; small mouth; last rays of dorsal fin form a long thread; younger fish have a dark spot behind the gill flap

Similar Species: Alewife (pg. 56), Goldeye/Mooneye (pp. 76-79)

Gizzard Shad	**Alewife**	**Gizzard Shad**	**Goldeye/ Mooneye**
anal fin typically 27 to 34 rays	anal fin typically 17 or 18 rays	scaled, saw-like keel	fleshy keel

GIZZARD SHAD

Dorosoma cepedianum

Clupeidae

Other Names: hickory, mud or jack shad, skipjack

Habitat: large rivers, reservoirs, lakes, swamps; brackish and saline waters in coastal areas

Range: St. Lawrence River and Great Lakes, Mississippi, Atlantic and Gulf Slope drainages from Quebec to Mexico, south to central Florida; in Wisconsin, Lake Michigan, Huron and Erie drainages

Food: herbivorous filter feeder

Reproduction: spawning takes place in tributary streams and along lakeshores in early summer; eggs and milt are released in schools, without regard for individual mates

Average Size: 6 to 8 inches, 1 to 8 ounces

Records: State—4 pounds, 7 ounces; Lake Michigan, Ozaukee County, 1982; North American—4 pounds, 12 ounces, Lake Oahe, South Dakota, 2006

Notes: The Gizzard Shad is a widespread, prolific fish that is best known as forage for popular game fish. At times it can become over-abundant and experience large die-offs. The name "gizzard" refers to its long, convoluted intestine, which is often packed with sand. Though Gizzard Shad are a management problem at times they form a valuable link in turning plankton into usable forage for large predators. Occasionally larger Gizzard Shad are caught with hook and line, but they have little food value.

CHESTNUT LAMPREY

Description: eel-like body with round, sucking-disk mouth and seven paired gill openings; dorsal fin is long, extending to the tail; no paired fins.

Similar Species: Sea Lamprey (pg. 62), Bowfin (pg. 32), Burbot (pg. 46), American Eel (pg. 50)

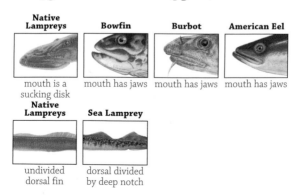

Native Lampreys	Bowfin	Burbot	American Eel
mouth is a sucking disk	mouth has jaws	mouth has jaws	mouth has jaws

Native Lampreys	Sea Lamprey
undivided dorsal fin	dorsal divided by deep notch

NATIVE LAMPREYS

Ichthyomyzon, Lampetra

Other Names: Silver, Chestnut, Northern Brook and American Brook Lamprey

Habitat: juveniles live in the quiet pools of streams and rivers; adults may move into some lakes

Range: freshwater of eastern North America; in Wisconsin primarily stream dwellers distributed throughout Wisconsin, but each species has a fairly restricted range within the state

Food: juvenile lampreys are filter feeders in stream bottoms; adults are either parasitic on fish or do not feed

Reproduction: adults build nest in the gravel of streambeds, typically after water temperatures reach about 55 degrees, then die shortly after spawning

Average Size: 6 to 12 inches

Records: none

Notes: There are four small, native lampreys found in Wisconsin. The Silver and Chestnut Lampreys are parasitic on fish in their adult form; the Northern Brook, and American Brook Lampreys are non-parasitic (adults do not feed). Unlike the introduced Sea Lamprey, native lampreys coexist with little impact on other Wisconsin fish populations. Lampreys are some of Earth's oldest vertebrates, with fossil records dating back 500 million years.

Description: eel-like body; round, sucking-disk mouth; seven paired gill openings; dorsal fin extends to the tail and is divided into two sections by a deep notch; no paired fins

Similar Species: Native Lampreys (pg. 60), Bowfin (pg. 32), Burbot (pg. 46), American Eel (pg. 50),

Sea Lamprey	Bowfin	Burbot	American Eel
mouth is a sucking disk	mouth has jaws	mouth has jaws	mouth has jaws

Sea Lamprey	Native Lampreys
dorsal fin divided by deep notch	undivided dorsal fin

SEA LAMPREY
Petromyzon marinus

Other Names: landlocked or lake lamprey

Habitat: juveniles live in quiet pools of freshwater streams; adults are free-swimming in lakes or oceans

Range: Atlantic Ocean from Greenland to Florida, Norway to the Mediterranean; the Great Lakes, in Wisconsin, lakes Superior and Michigan and some of their tributaries

Food: juvenile form is a filter feeder in the bottom of streams; adult is parasitic on fish, attaching itself using disk-shaped sucker mouth and sharp teeth, then using its sharp tongue to rasp through the fish's scales and skin to feed on blood and bodily fluids; many "host" fish die

Reproduction: both adults build a nest in the gravel of a clear stream, then die shortly after spawning; young remain in stream several years before returning to the lake as adults

Average Size: 12 to 24 inches

Records: none

Notes: Native to the Atlantic Ocean, the Sea Lamprey entered the Great Lakes via the St. Lawrence Seaway. It was initially blocked by Niagara Falls, but when the Welland Canal allowed it to bypass the falls, it entered the upper Great Lakes. The first was recorded from Lake Superior in 1936. Two years later one was found in Lake Michigan. Soon after, the Lake Trout and Whitefish populations began to decline. With the use of traps and chemicals, the Sea Lamprey population is now under partial control.

BIGHEAD CARP

Description: large body; upturned mouth without barbels; low-set eyes; small scales on body, none on the head

Similar Species: Common Carp (pg. 66), Buffalo (pp. 124-129)

Asian Carp	**Common Carp**	**Buffalo**
upturned mouth lacks barbels; eyes low on head	down-turned mouth with barbels	eyes set high on head

ASIAN CARP:

bighead, black, grass and silver carp

Ctenopharyngodon, Hypophthalmichthys

Other Names: carp, flyers, jumpers

Habitat: large, warm rivers and connected lakes

Range: native to Asia, introduced in other parts of the world; in Wisconsin, the Mississippi River

Food: aquatic vegetation, floating plankton

Reproduction: research in colonized waters is limited, but indicates that Asian Carp spawn from late spring to early summer in warm, flowing water, often in headwaters of tributary streams

Average Size: 16 to 22 inches, 5 to 50 pounds

Records: Grass Carp, North American—80 pounds, Lake Wedington, Arkansas, 2004; Bighead Carp, North American—90 pounds, Kirby Lake, Texas, 2000

Notes: Introduced into the U.S. to control algae in southern aquaculture ponds, these four species of Asian carp eventually escaped to the Mississippi River—a natural highway for invading new territory. The Black and Grass Carp do not threaten Wisconsin waters at this time, but the Silver and Bighead Carp—voracious plankton feeders with the potential to disrupt the entire food web—pose a serious risk. The Silver Carp, and to a lesser degree the Bighead, make high leaps from the water when frightened by boats, occasionally injuring boaters.

Description: two pairs of barbels near round, extendable mouth; brassy yellow to golden brown or dark-olive sides; white belly; some red on tail and anal fin; each scale has a dark spot at the base and a dark margin

Similar Species: Asian Carp (pg. 64), Buffalo (pp. 124-129), Quillback (pg. 130)

Common Carp	**Asian Carp**	**Buffalo**	**Quillback**
down-turned mouth with barbels, eyes high on head	upturned mouth lacks barbels, eyes low on head	lacks barbels	lacks barbels

COMMON CARP

Cyprinus carpio

Cyprinidae

Other Names: German, European, mirror or leather carp, buglemouth

Habitat: warm, shallow, quiet, well-vegetated waters of both streams and lakes

Range: native to Asia; introduced throughout the world; in Wisconsin, common in the Mississippi and Lake Michigan drainages; rare in the Lake Superior drainage

Food: prefers insects, crustaceans and mollusks but at times eats algae and other plants

Reproduction: spawns from late spring to early summer in very shallow water at stream and lake edges; spawning adults are easily seen due to energetic splashing along shore

Average Size: 16 to 18 inches, 5 to 20 pounds

Records: State—57 pounds, 2 ounces; Lake Washington, Columbia County, 1966; North American—57 pounds, 13 ounces; Tidal Basin, Washington D.C., 1983

Notes: Though despised by some Wisconsin anglers, the Common Carp is one of the world's most important freshwater fish, providing food and sport for millions of people throughout its range. This fast-growing Asian minnow was introduced into Europe in the twelfth century but didn't make it to North America until the 1870s. In 1880, seventy-five carp were brought from Washington, D.C. to the Nevin Hatchery in Madison; from that humble beginning, carp have become the most widespread large fish in the state.

67

Description: gray to olive brown, often with a dark stripe on side and black spot at the base of tail; red spot behind eye; breeding males develop hornlike tubercles on the head

Similar Species: Fathead Minnow (pg. 72), Creek Chub

Hornyhead Chub	Fathead Minnow	Creek Chub
down-turned mouth extends to eye	upturned mouth does not extend to eye	mouth extends to middle of eye

HORNYHEAD CHUB
Nocomis biguttatus

Cyprinidae

Other Names: redtail, horned or river chub

Habitat: small to medium-size streams, and occasionally in lakes near stream mouths

Range: northern Midwest through the Great Lakes region; very common throughout Wisconsin

Food: small aquatic invertebrates, zooplankton

Reproduction: in late spring male excavates a 1- to 3-foot diameter pit in gravelly stream riffle, then fills it with small stones (carried in by mouth), creating a 6- to 8-inch-high mound; females lay eggs on the mound; male covers fertilized eggs with gravel; other species such as Common Shiner may also use the mound for spawning, and some research suggests the two males cooperate to defend the nest

Average Size: 4 to 12 inches

Records: none

Notes: In Wisconsin there are five larger minnows we call chubs. The Creek and Hornyhead grow to a foot long and can be caught with hook and line. The Hornyhead is a common bait minnow, often called Redtail Chub. In situations such as fall Walleye fishing it is the preferred bait, outfishing other species such as Common Shiner by a wide margin. Due to high demand, anglers sometimes pay $8 or more per dozen, making it costlier per pound than lobster.

Description: moderately dark back; two broad lateral bands on tan background; in breeding males, the tan turns orange and the belly becomes bright red or orange; blunt nose

Similar Species: Southern Redbelly Dace, Finescale Dace

Northern Redbelly Dace

curved mouth, lower jaw slightly ahead of upper

Southern Redbelly Dace

straight mouth, upper jaw slightly ahead of the lower

Northern Redbelly Dace

two dark lateral stripes

Finescale Dace

single dark lateral stripe

NORTHERN REDBELLY DACE

Cyprinidae

Phoxinus eos

Other Names: redbelly, leatherback, yellow-belly dace

Habitat: small streams and bog lakes

Range: Northwest Territories to Hudson Bay, northeastern US and eastern Canada; in Wisconsin, present in all three drainage basins, but rare or absent in the unglaciated southwestern quarter of Wisconsin; rarely seen in lakes Superior and Michigan

Food: bottom feeder that primarily eats plant material

Reproduction: from May to early August, a single female accompanied by several males will dart among masses of filamentous algae, laying 5 to 30 non-adhesive eggs at a time; males fertilize the eggs, which hatch in 8 to 10 days with no parental care

Average Size: 2 to 3 inches

Records: none

Notes: There are eight species of minnows in Wisconsin that are referred to as daces, including the Blacknose, Finescale, Longnose, Pearl, Redside and Southern Redbelly. These are small fish that live in a variety of habitats. The Northern Redbelly Dace is a hardy fish often found in the acidic water of bog-stained lakes and beaver ponds, and occasionally sold as bait in northern Wisconsin. Breeding males are one of Wisconsin's brightest colored fish and surpass many aquarium fish for beauty.

Description: olive back, golden yellow sides and white belly; dark lateral line widens to spot at base of tail; rounded snout and fins; no scales on head; dark blotch on dorsal fin

Similar Species: Hornyhead Chub (pg. 68), Creek Chub

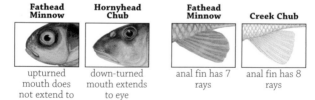

Fathead Minnow	Hornyhead Chub	Fathead Minnow	Creek Chub
upturned mouth does not extend to eye	down-turned mouth extends to eye	anal fin has 7 rays	anal fin has 8 rays

FATHEAD MINNOW
Pemephales promelas

Other Names: fathead, blackhead, tuffy, mudminnow

Habitat: streams, ponds and lakes, particularly shallow, weedy or turbid (cloudy) areas lacking predators

Range: east of the Rocky Mountains in the U. S. and Canada; found throughout Wisconsin

Food: primarily herbivorous but will eat insects and copepods

Reproduction: from the time water temperatures reach 60 degrees in spring through August, male prepares nest under rocks and sticks; female enters, turns upside down and lays adhesive eggs on the overhead object; after the female leaves, the male fertilizes the eggs, which it then guards, fans with its fins and massages with a special, mucus-like pad on its back

Average Size: 3 to 4 inches

Records: none

Notes: Minnows are small fish, not the young of larger species. The Fathead is one of our most numerous and widespread fish, commonly used as bait. It is hardy and withstands extremely low oxygen levels—both in the wild and in bait buckets. Prior to spawning, the male develops a dark coloration, breeding tubercles on its head that resemble small horns, and a mucus-like patch on its back; during this phase, anglers report having better luck when using female Fatheads, perhaps due to their color or differing scent.

Description: silver body with dark green back, often with a dark body stripe; breeding males have bluish heads and rosy pink on body and fins

Similar Species: Golden Shiner (pg. 74), Creek Chub

Common Shiner	**Golden Shiner**	**Common Shiner**	**Creek Chub**
8 to 10 rays on anal fin (usually 9)	11 to 15 rays on anal fin	mouth barely extends to eye, which is large in relation to head	mouth extends almost to middle of eye, which is small in relation to head

COMMON SHINER
Notropis cornutus

Cyprinidae

Other Names: common, eastern, creek or redfin shiner

Habitat: lakes, rivers and streams; most common in the pools of streams and small rivers

Range: Midwest through eastern U.S. and Canada; common in all three Wisconsin drainage basins

Food: small insects, algae, zooplankton

Reproduction: beginning in late May, male prepares nest of small stones and gravel at the head of a stream riffle (sometimes using the nest of a Creek Chub or Hornyhead Chub); other males are chased away, but females are courted with great flourish; it is generally thought that after spawning, both male and female abandon the nest, but research has documented male Common Shiners and Hornyhead Chubs cooperating to defend a nest

Average Size: 4 to 12 inches

Records: none

Notes: Not all shiners are as flashy as the name indicates. Some are dull-colored and show almost no silver on the sides. The Common Shiner is one of the larger native Wisconsin minnows, occasionally reaching 12 inches in length. It has now replaced the Golden Shiner as the common bait shiner, though it seems somewhat less hardy on the hook. Large Common Shiners can be caught on dry flies and are occasionally eaten; though not as meaty as panfish, they are every bit as tenacious when hooked.

Description: dark blue to dark green back and upper sides; bright silver or golden sides; large scales; large, yellow-tinged eye; thin body, flattened from side to side with a sharp, scaleless ridge (keel) ahead of the pelvic fin; forward-facing (terminal) mouth with small teeth

Similar Species: Mooneye (pg. 78), Gizzard Shad (pg. 58)

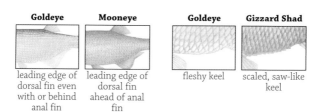

Goldeye	Mooneye	Goldeye	Gizzard Shad
leading edge of dorsal fin even with or behind anal fin	leading edge of dorsal fin ahead of anal fin	fleshy keel	scaled, saw-like keel

GOLDEYE
Hiodon alosoides

Hiodontidae

Other Names: Winnipeg or western goldeye, toothed or yellow herring

Habitat: large lakes and quiet areas of turbid (cloudy) rivers, including backwaters and connected lakes

Range: Hudson Bay drainage south through the Ohio and Mississippi drainage to Tennessee; in Wisconsin, only occurs in the Mississippi River, and the lower St. Croix, Chippewa and Wisconsin rivers

Food: insects, small fish, crayfish, snails

Reproduction: spawning takes place in turbid pools and backwaters when water temperatures reach the mid-50s

Average Size: 12 to 17 inches, 1 to 2 pounds

Records: State—none; North American—3 pounds, 13 ounces; Lake Oahe Tailwater, South Dakota, 1987

Notes: The Goldeye's large, yellow eye is an adaptation for low-light conditions, enabling it to feed at night and navigate dark, silty waters. It feeds in quiet water near the surface, often near Mooneyes. Harvested commercially from large Canadian lakes for more than 150 years, it was served on the Canadian Pacific Railway as Winnipeg Smoked Goldeye. It was once an important commercial species on Lake of the Woods and the Red Lakes as well. The Goldeye is fun to catch on hook and line, but few anglers target it.

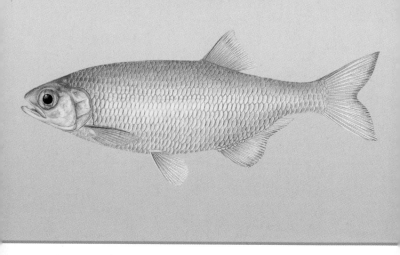

Description: silver with olive back; large scales on body but none on the head; large, white eye more than one third the width of head; thin body with a sharp scale-less keel between pelvic and anal fins

Similar Species: Goldeye (pg. 76), Gizzard Shad (pg. 58)

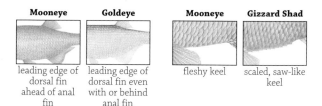

Mooneye	**Goldeye**	**Mooneye**	**Gizzard Shad**
leading edge of dorsal fin ahead of anal fin	leading edge of dorsal fin even with or behind anal fin	fleshy keel	scaled, saw-like keel

MOONEYE

Hiodon tergisus

Other Names: white shad, slicker, toothed herring, river whitefish

Habitat: clear, quiet waters of large lakes and the backwaters of large streams

Range: Hudson Bay drainage east to the St. Lawrence, through the Mississippi drainage south into Arkansas and Alabama; in Wisconsin, the Mississippi River and its larger tributaries; Green Bay and some of its tributaries

Food: insects, small fish, crayfish, snails

Reproduction: spawning takes place in clear backwaters and over rocks in swift-water areas when water temperatures reach the mid-50s; a single female may release up to 20,000 gelatin-covered eggs

Average Size: 12 inches, 12 to 16 ounces

Records: State—1 pound, 9 ounces; Lake Winnebago, Winnebago County, 1999; North American—1 pound, 12 ounces; Lake Poygan, Wisconsin, 2000

Notes: The Mooneye is a flashy fish that jumps repeatedly when hooked. However, it is bony, with little meat except along the back, and is not a good table fish. It commonly feeds on insects at or near the surface in slack waters of large lakes and rivers. Because it requires clean, clear water it is becoming less common due to the siltation of many streams. Though small, it is related to the South American Arapaima, the world's largest scaled freshwater fish.

Description: large, gray scale-less body; snout protrudes into a large paddle; shark-like forked tail; gills extend into long, pointed flaps

Similar Species: Channel Catfish (pg. 40), Blue Catfish

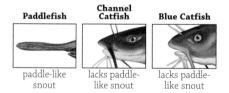

Paddlefish	**Channel Catfish**	**Blue Catfish**
paddle-like snout	lacks paddle-like snout	lacks paddle-like snout

PADDLEFISH
Polyodon spathula

Other Names: spoonbill cat, duckbill

Habitat: deep pools of large rivers and their connecting lakes

Range: large rivers in the Mississippi drainage; in Wisconsin, the lower Mississippi and St. Croix rivers; most common in Lake St. Croix and Lake Pepin

Food: free-swimming plankton

Reproduction: spawning takes place when water levels are rising and water temperatures reach the low 50s; adults migrate from lakes and rivers into streams; breeding schools gather to release eggs over large gravel bars, typically in less than 10 feet of water; a female may lay up to 600,000 eggs

Average Size: 24 to 48 inches, 30 to 50 pounds

Records: State—none; North American—144 pounds; Dam No. 7, Kansas, 2004

Notes: This prehistoric fish is very shark-like in anatomy, with its only close relative found in the Yangtze River of China. Paddlefish have a large mouth but no teeth and feed entirely on plankton. The function of the paddle is not well understood but it is not used to dig in the mud. In fact, scientists believe special sensors in the snout help the Paddlefish detect tiny electrical currents created by groups of the plankton on which it feeds. With increased pollution and silting in the Mississippi River, paddlefish are now rare in Wisconsin but were once common and a prized food fish.

IOWA DARTER

JOHNNY
DARTER

Description: Iowa Darter—brown back with faint blotches; sides have 9 to 12 vertical bars; dark spot under eye; bars become more pronounced and colors brighter on breeding males; Johnny Darter—tan to olive back and upper sides with dark blotches and speckling; sides tan to golden with X, Y and W patterns; breeding males dark with black bars

Similar Species: Iowa Darter; Johnny Darter

Iowa Darter   **Johnny Darter**

blotches or bars on sides   X, Y and W markings on sides

IOWA DARTER *Etheostoma exile*
JOHNNY DARTER *Etheostoma nigrum*

Other Names: red-sided, yellowbelly or weed darter

Habitat: Iowa Darters inhabit slow-flowing streams and lakes that have some vegetation or an algae mat; Johnny Darters are found in most rivers, streams and lakes

Range: Rocky Mountains east across Canada and the U.S. through the Great Lakes region; some species of darter can be found in most of the streams in Wisconsin; the Iowa darter is common in all three Wisconsin drainage basins

Food: waterfleas, insect larvae

Reproduction: in May and June, males migrate to shorelines to establish breeding areas; females move from territory to territory, spawning with several males; each sequence produces 7 to 10 eggs, which sink and attach to the bottom

Average Size: 2 to 4 inches

Records: none

Notes: Darters are primarily stream fish, adapted to living among the rocks in fast current. They have very small swim bladders, allowing them to sink rapidly to the bottom after a "dart," thus avoiding being swept away by the current. There are about a dozen species of darters in Wisconsin. The Iowa Darter is a lake species that inhabits weedy shoreline areas. It is hard to see when still, but easy to spot when it makes a quick dart to a new resting place. Iowa Darters make fine aquarium fish, but require live food. Males lose much of their color in captivity.

Description: slender body; gray to dark silver or yellowish brown with dark blotches on sides; black spots on spiny dorsal fin; may exhibit some white on lower margin of tail, but lacks prominent white spot found on Walleye

Similar Species: Walleye (pg. 86)

Sauger	**Walleye**	**Sauger**	**Walleye**
no white spot on tail	white spot on bottom of tail	spiny dorsal fin is spotted, lacks dark blotch on rear base	spiny dorsal fin lacks spots, has large dark spot on rear base

SAUGER
Sander canadensis

Other Names: sand pike, spotfin pike, river pike, jackfish, jack salmon

Habitat: large lakes and rivers

Range: large lakes in southern Canada, northern U.S. and the larger reaches of the Mississippi, Missouri, Ohio and Tennessee River drainages; in Wisconsin, Mississippi River drainage, Green Bay, lower Fox River and Lake Winnebago

Food: small fish, aquatic insects, crayfish

Reproduction: spawns in April and May as water approaches 50 degrees; adults move into the shallow waters of tributaries and headwaters to randomly deposit eggs over gravel beds

Average Size: 12 to 13 inches, 8 ounces to 2 pounds

Records: State—5 pounds, 13 ounces; Lake Wisconsin, Columbia County, 1988; North American—8 pounds, 12 ounces; Lake Sakakawea, North Dakota, 1971

Notes: Saugeye are hatchery produced hybrids crossing Walleye and Sauger. Though the Sauger is the Walleye's smaller cousin it is a big-water fish primarily found in large lakes and rivers. It is slow growing, often reaching only 2 pounds in 20 years. An important sport fish on Wisconsin waters including Lake Winnebago and the lower Mississippi River, it is an aggressive daytime feeder compared to the Walleye. Its fine-flavored fillets are top table fare.

Description: long, round body; dark silver or golden to dark olive brown in color; spines in both first dorsal and anal fin; sharp canine teeth; dark spot at base of the three last spines in the dorsal fin; white spot on bottom lobe of tail

Similar Species: Sauger (pg. 84)

Walleye	**Sauger**	**Walleye**	**Sauger**
white spot on bottom of tail	no white spot on tail	spiny dorsal fin lacks spots, has large dark spot on rear base	spiny dorsal fin is spotted, lacks dark blotch on rear base

WALLEYE
Sander vitreus

Other Names: marble-eyes, 'eye, walleyed pike, jack, pickerel

Habitat: lakes and streams, abundant in very large lakes

Range: originally the northern states and Canada, now widely stocked in the U.S.; historically found only in larger Wisconsin lakes and streams; now common throughout the state

Food: mainly small fish, but also eats insects, crayfish, leeches and other small prey as opportunity permits

Reproduction: spawning takes place in tributary streams or rocky lake shoals when spring water temperatures reach 45 to 50 degrees; no parental care

Average Size: 14 to 17 inches, 1 to 3 pounds

Records: State—18 pounds, High Lake, Vilas County, 1933; North American—22 pounds, 11 ounces, Greer's Ferry Lake, Arkansas, 1982

Notes: Revered by anglers. Not a spectacular fighter, but it ranks high in table quality. One- to 3-pound fish are excellent eating; breaking the 10-pound mark is a milestone in most fishing careers. A reflective layer of pigment in the eye, called *tapetum lucidum*, allows it to see well in low-light conditions, giving it an advantage over prey species such as Yellow Perch, which have poorer night vision or cannot quickly adapt to reduced light levels. As a result, Walleyes (particularly in clear lakes) are often most active at dusk, dawn, night and in light-reducing conditions such as waves or heavy cloud cover.

Description: 6 to 9 dark, vertical bars on bright yellowish green to orange background; long dorsal fin with two distinct lobes; lower fins have a yellow to orange tinge

Similar Species: Trout-perch (pg. 164), Walleye (pg. 86)

Yellow Perch	**Trout-perch**	**Yellow Perch**	**Walleye**
no adipose fin	adipose fin	lacks prominent white spot on tail	prominent white spot on tail

YELLOW PERCH
Perca flavescens

Other Names: ringed, striped or jack perch, green hornet

Habitat: lakes and streams preferring clear open water

Range: widely introduced throughout southern Canada and northern U.S.; common throughout Wisconsin except in the southwest corner

Food: small fish, insects, snails, leeches and crayfish

Reproduction: spawns at night in shallow, weedy areas after ice-out when water warms to 45 degrees; female drapes gelatinous ribbons of eggs over submerged vegetation

Average Size: 8 to 11 inches, 6 to 10 ounces

Records: State—3 pounds, 4 ounces; Lake Winnebago, Winnebago County, 1954; North American—4 pounds, 3 ounces; Delaware River, New Jersey, 1865

Notes: The Yellow Perch is very common, and possibly the most popular sport and food fish in Wisconsin. With simple tackle even inexperienced anglers can be successful at perch fishing. Anglers on Lake Mendota have caught a million and a half perch in a single ice-fishing season. The Lake Michigan perch population has been adversely affected by alewives, but the lake still supports a strong recreational fishery. In smaller inland lakes, the overfishing of top predators can lead to a population of stunted perch.

MUSKELLUNGE

TIGER MUSKIE

Description: torpedo-shaped body; dorsal fin near tail; sides typically silver to silver-green with dark spots or bars on light background; pointed lobes on tail; lower half of gill cover has no scales

Similar Species: Northern Pike (pg. 92), Tiger Muskie

Muskellunge	Northern Pike	Muskellunge	Northern Pike
dark marks on light background	light marks on dark background	6 or more pores on each side under the jaw	5 or fewer pores each side under the jaw

Muskellunge	Northern Pike	Tiger Muskie
pointed tail	rounded tail	rounded tail

MUSKELLUNGE

Esox masquinongy

Other Names: musky, muskie, 'ski, lunge

Habitat: large, clear lakes with extensive weedbeds; also medium to large rivers with slow currents and deep pools

Range: Great Lakes east to Maine, south through Ohio River drainage to Tennessee; introduced statewide, most common in north-central Wisconsin in the Chippewa, Flambeau and St. Croix drainages, and in the Wisconsin and Black rivers

Food: small fish, occasionally muskrats, ducklings

Reproduction: spawns mid-April to May at 50- to 60-degree water temperatures; eggs are laid in dead vegetation in tributaries, or in shallow bays with muck bottoms; male and female swim side by side for several hundred yards, depositing fertilized eggs; larval Muskellunge are often preyed upon by young Northern Pike, which hatch about 2 weeks earlier

Average Size: 30 to 42 inches, 10 to 20 pounds

Records: State—69 pounds, 11 ounces; Chippewa Flowage, Sawyer County, 1949; North American—69 pounds, 11 ounces; Chippewa Flowage, Wisconsin, 1949

Notes: Named Wisconsin's state fish in 1955, the Muskellunge is a sought-after trophy. More than 700 lakes and 83 streams in 48 counties contain fishable populations, but it still takes more than 50 hours on average to catch a legal fish. It is thinly dispersed—typically one fish every two or three acres—and hard to entice with live bait or lures. Naturally hybridizes with Northern Pike to form the Tiger Muskie.

Description: long body with dorsal fin near tail; head is long and flattened in front, forming a duck-like snout; dark green back, light green sides with bean-shaped light spots; Silver Pike are a rare, silver colored race of Northern Pike

Similar Species: Muskellunge (pg. 90), Tiger Muskie (pg. 90)

Northern Pike	**Muskellunge**	**Tiger Muskie**
light spots on dark background	dark marks on light background	dark marks on light background

Northern Pike	**Muskellunge**	**Northern Pike**	**Muskellunge**
rounded tail	pointed tail	five or fewer pores on underside of jaw	6 or more pores on each side under the jaw

NORTHERN PIKE

Esox lucius

Other Names: pickerel, jack, gator, hammerhandle, snot rocket

Habitat: lakes, ponds, streams and rivers; often found near weeds; small pike tolerate water temperatures up to 70 degrees but larger fish prefer cooler water, 55 degrees or less

Range: northern Europe, Asia and North America; in Wisconsin, common throughout the state, and in the shallows of both Great Lakes

Food: small fish, occasionally frogs, crayfish

Reproduction: late March to early April in tributaries and marshes at 34- to 40-degree water temperatures; attended by 1 to 3 males, female deposits eggs in shallow vegetation

Average Size: 18 to 24 inches, 2 to 5 pounds

Records: State—38 pounds; Lake Puckaway, Green County, 1952; North American—46 pounds, 2 ounces; Sacandaga Reservoir, New York, 1940

Notes: This large, fast predator is one of the most widespread freshwater fish in the world and a prime sport fish throughout its range. Its long, tube-shaped body and intra-muscular bones are adaptations for quick bursts of speed in pursuit of prey. Northern Pike have firm, white flesh that can become fishy tasting if allowed contact with the pike's outer slime. They willingly hit a variety of live and artificial baits, and fight hard when hooked. The Tiger Muskellunge is a northern pike muskellunge hybrid, and is considered a Muskellunge in bag limits.

Description: back is olive, blue-gray to black with wormlike markings; sides bronze to olive with red spots tinged light brown; lower fins red-orange with white leading edge; tail squared or slightly forked

Similar Species: Brown Trout (pg. 96), Rainbow Trout (pg. 100), Lake Trout (pg. 98), Splake (pg. 98)

Brook Trout	Brown Trout	Rainbow Trout	Lake Trout
worm-like marks, red spots	large dark spots, small red dots	pink stripe on silver body	sides lack red spots

Brook Trout	Lake Trout	Splake
tail square to slightly forked	tail deeply forked	tail moderately forked

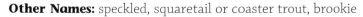

BROOK TROUT
Salvelinus fontinalis

Other Names: speckled, squaretail or coaster trout, brookie

Habitat: cool, clear streams and small lakes with sand or gravel bottoms and moderate vegetation; coastal Lake Superior; prefers water temperatures of 50 to 60 degrees

Range: Great Lakes north to Labrador, south through the Appalachians to Georgia; introduced into the western U.S., Canada, Europe and South America; occurs naturally in the streams of all three Wisconsin drainages, in some deeper inland lakes and Lake Superior

Food: insects, small fish, leeches, crustaceans

Reproduction: spawns in late fall at 40- to 49-degree water temperatures on gravel bars in stream riffles and in lakes where springs aerate eggs; female builds 4- to 12-inch-deep nest (male may guard during construction) in gravel, then buries fertilized eggs, which hatch in 50 to 150 days

Average Size: 8 to 10 inches, 8 ounces

Records: State—10 pounds, 1 ounce, Lake Michigan, Ozaukee County, 1999; North American—14 pounds, 8 ounces, Nipigon River, Ontario, 1916

Notes: The Brook Trout is the only native stream trout in Wisconsin. This small, beautiful trout—with its voracious appetite, strong runs and delicate flavor—epitomizes fishing in pristine waters. Though "coaster" brook trout found in Lake Superior are rare, they are highly prized by anglers and provide the best chance of catching a 2-pound brookie.

BROWN TROUT

TIGER TROUT

Description: golden-brown to olive back and sides; large dark spots on sides, dorsal fin and sometimes upper lobe of tail; red spots with light halos scattered along sides

Similar Species: Rainbow Trout (pg. 100), Lake Trout (pg. 98), Brook Trout (pg. 96), Tiger Trout

Brown Trout	**Rainbow Trout**	**Lake Trout**
dark spots on brown or olive	pink stripe on silvery body	white spots on dark background

Brown Trout	**Brook Trout**	**Tiger Trout**
lacks wormlike markings	wormlike markings on back	wormlike markings on back and sides

BROWN TROUT

Salmo trutta

Other Names: German brown, Loch Leven or spotted trout

Habitat: open ocean near its spawning streams and clear, cold, gravel-bottomed streams; shallow areas of Lake Superior

Range: native to Europe from the Mediterranean to Arctic Norway and Siberia, widely introduced worldwide; established in cold streams throughout Wisconsin, maintained through stocking in lakes Superior and Michigan

Food: insects, crayfish, small fish

Reproduction: spawns October through December in stream headwaters and tributaries; stream mouths are used when migration is blocked; female fans out saucer-shaped nest, which male guards until spawning; female covers eggs

Average Size: 11 to 20 inches, 2 to 6 pounds

Records: State—36 pounds, 8.9 ounces; Lake Michigan, Kewaunee County, 2004; North American—40 pounds, 4 ounces; Little Red River River, Arkansas, 1992

Notes: This European trout was brought to North America in 1883 and to Wisconsin in 1887. Brown Trout prefer cold spring-fed streams but will tolerate much warmer water and some turbidity better than other trout. A favorite of fly fishermen around the world, browns are secretive, hard-to-catch fish. It is not uncommon for them to hybridize with Brook Trout; the Tiger Trout is the colorful but sterile offspring of this cross.

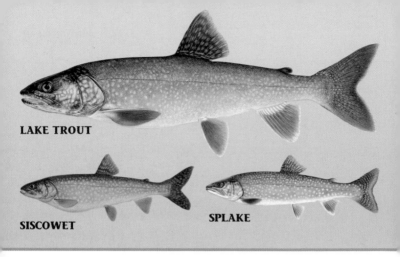

LAKE TROUT

SISCOWET

SPLAKE

Description: dark gray to gray-green on head, back, top fins and tail; white spots on sides and unpaired fins; deeply forked tail; inside of mouth is white

Similar Species: Brook Trout (pg. 94), Splake, Siscowet

Lake Trout	**Brook Trout**	**Lake Trout**	**Siscowet**
sides lack wormlike markings	wormlike marks on back	body length greater than 4 times depth	length less than 4 times body depth

Lake Trout	**Brook Trout**	**Splake**
tail deeply forked	tail square to slightly forked	tail moderately forked

LAKE TROUT
Salvelinus namaycush

Other Names: togue, mackinaw, great gray trout, laker

Habitat: cold (less than 65 degrees), oxygen-rich waters of deep, clear, infertile lakes

Range: Great Lakes north through Canada, to northeastern U.S., stocked in the Rocky Mountains; in Wisconsin, deep, cold lakes of all three drainage systems, and in lakes Superior and Michigan

Food: small fish, insects

Reproduction: females scatter eggs over rocky lake bottoms when fall water temperature falls below 50 degrees

Average Size: 15 to 20 inches, 7 to 10 pounds

Records: State—47 pounds, Lake Superior, Bayfield County, 1946; North American—72 pounds, 4 ounces, Great Bear Lake, N.W.T., Canada, 1995

Notes: The Lake Trout is the largest trout and native to Wisconsin. From the 1890s to the 1940s it was an important commercial species, but the fishery was decimated in the mid-1950s by overfishing and the introduction of the Sea Lamprey. With vigorous stocking and lamprey control, Lake Trout have returned to levels that support recreational fishing. However, natural reproduction is decreasing in many lakes. A high-fat subspecies called the Siscowet (*Salvelinus namaycush siscowet*) or "fat" Lake Trout inhabits the deep waters of Lake Superior and may spend its life in water no warmer than 40 degrees.

Description: blue-green to brown head and back; silver lower sides, often with pink to rose stripe; sides, back, dorsal fins and tail are covered with small black spots

Similar Species: Brown Trout (pg. 96), Brook Trout (pg. 94), Pink Salmon (pg. 106), Chinook Salmon (pg. 102)

Rainbow Trout

pinkish stripe on silvery body

Brown Trout

sides lack pinkish stripe

Rainbow Trout

lacks wormlike markings

Brook Trout

wormlike marks on back

Rainbow Trout

white mouth

Pink Salmon

dark tongue and jaw tip

Chinook Salmon

black or dark gray mouth

RAINBOW TROUT

Oncorhynchus mykiss

Other Names: steelhead, Pacific trout, silver trout, 'bow

Habitat: prefers whitewater in cool streams and coastal regions of large lakes, tolerates smaller cool, clear lakes

Range: Pacific Ocean and coastal streams from Mexico to Alaska and northeast Russia, introduced worldwide including the Great Lakes, eastern U.S. and southern Canada; introduced into cooler streams and lakes throughout Wisconsin

Food: insects, small crustaceans, fish

Reproduction: predominantly spring spawners but some fall-spawning varieties have been introduced in Wisconsin; female builds nest in well-aerated gravel in streams and lakes

Average Size: 20 inches, 3 to 8 pounds

Records: State—27 pounds, 2 ounces; Lake Michigan, Kewaunee County, 1997; North American—42 pounds, 2 ounces, Bell Island, Alaska, 1970

Notes: A popular, hard-fighting game fish, the Rainbow Trout was brought to Wisconsin in the 1800s from the Pacific Northwest. They reproduce in some lakes and streams across the state, including Lake Superior, but much of the fishery is maintained by stocking. Rainbows tolerate warm water better than other trout; some varieties survive temperatures in the low 80s. A migratory strain of rainbow called steelhead lives in the Pacific Ocean, then migrates into streams to spawn; steelhead introduced into the Great Lakes reside in the lakes and spawn in tributaries.

Description: iridescent green to blue-green back and upper sides; silver below lateral line; small spots on back and tail; inside of mouth is dark; breeding males are olive brown to purple with pronounced kype (hooked snout)

Similar Species: Coho Salmon (pg. 104), Pink Salmon (pg. 106), Rainbow Trout (pg. 100)

Chinook Salmon

small spots throughout tail

Coho Salmon

spots only in top half of tail

Pink Salmon

eye-sized spots throughout tail

Chinook Salmon

inside of mouth is dark

Coho Salmon

inside of mouth is gray

Rainbow Trout

inside of mouth is white

CHINOOK SALMON

Oncorhynchus tshawytscha

Salmonidae

Other Names: king, spring salmon, tyee, quinnat, black mouth

Habitat: open ocean and large, clear, gravel-bottomed rivers, open water of lakes Superior and Michigan and associated spawning streams

Range: Pacific Ocean from California to Japan, introduced to the Atlantic coast in Maine; in Wisconsin, lakes Superior and Michigan

Food: fish (especially smelt and ciscoes), crustaceans

Reproduction: chinooks in the Great Lakes mature in 3 to 5 years; in October and November they migrate up streams to attempt nesting on gravel bars; adults die shortly after

Average Size: 24 to 30 inches, 15 to 20 pounds

Records: State—44 pounds, 15 ounces; Lake Michigan, Door County, 1994; North American—97 pounds, 4 ounces; Kenai River, Alaska, 1985

Notes: Largest member of the salmon family, chinooks may reach 40 pounds in landlocked lakes and can get much larger in the Pacific; the late-maturing strain that spawns in Alaska's Kenai River often tops 60 pounds and produced the world record of nearly 100. A renowned fighter prized as table fare, the Chinook is popular with anglers. Wisconsin followed Michigan's initial 1965 stocking with a program of its own in 1969. The introduction was very successful in creating the most important sport fishery in Wisconsin. A "put-and-take" fish; with little or no natural reproduction in the Great Lakes.

Description: dark metallic blue to green back; silver sides and belly; small dark spots on back, sides and upper half of tail; inside of mouth is gray; breeding adults gray to green on head with red-maroon sides, males develop kype (hooked snout)

Similar Species: Chinook Salmon (pg. 102), Pink Salmon (pg. 106), Rainbow Trout (pg. 100)

Coho Salmon	**Chinook Salmon**	**Pink Salmon**

spots only in top half of tail	small spots throughout tail	eye-sized spots throughout tail

Coho Salmon	**Rainbow Trout**
inside of mouth is gray	inside of mouth is white

COHO SALMON
Oncorhynchus kisutch

Other Names: silver salmon, sea trout, blueback

Habitat: open ocean near clear, gravel-bottomed spawning streams, Lake Superior within 10 miles of shore

Range: Pacific Ocean north from California to Japan, Atlantic coast of U.S.; in Wisconsin, lakes Superior and Michigan

Food: smelt, alewives and other fish

Reproduction: spawns in October and November; adults migrate up tributary streams to build nests on gravel bars; parent fish die shortly after spawning

Average Size: 20 inches, 4 to 5 pounds

Records: State—26 pounds, 1.9 ounces; Lake Michigan, Milwaukee County, 1999; North American—33 pounds, 4 ounces; Salmon River, New York, 1989

Notes: A very strong fighter and excellent table fare, this Pacific salmon was first stocked in the Great Lakes by the Michigan Department of Natural Resources in 1965. Wisconsin started stocking Lake Michigan soon after. The result has been a thriving population of sport fish. Cohos do much better in the Wisconsin streams of Lake Superior than the cold Minnesota streams. They grow very fast in Lake Michigan and reach over 20 pounds when mature; Lake Superior cohos are smaller.

Salmon Family

Salmonidae

105

Description: steel blue to blue-green back with silver sides; dark spots on back and tail, some as large as the eye; breeding males develop a large hump in front of the dorsal fin and a hooked upper jaw (kype); both sexes are pink during spawn

Similar Species: Chinook Salmon (pg. 102), Coho Salmon (pg. 104), Brown Trout (pg. 96), Rainbow Trout (pg. 100)

Pink Salmon	**Chinook Salmon**	**Coho Salmon**
eye-sized spots throughout tail	small spots throughout tail	spots only in top half of tail

Pink Salmon	**Coho Salmon**	**Brown Trout**	**Rainbow Trout**
dark tongue and jaw tip	inside of mouth is gray	inside of mouth is white	inside of mouth is white

PINK SALMON

Oncorhynchus gorbuscha

Other Names: humpback salmon, humpy, autumn salmon

Habitat: Coastal Pacific Ocean and open water of the Great Lakes, spawns in clear streams

Range: coastal Pacific Ocean from northern California to Alaska, introduced to Great Lakes; Lake Superior and the mouth of clear steams during the spawning run; much less common in Lake Michigan and its tributaries

Food: small fish, crustaceans

Reproduction: spawns in fall in tributary streams, usually at two years of age; female builds nest on gravel bar, then covers fertilized eggs; adults die after spawning

Average Size: 17 to 19 inches, 1 to 2 pounds

Records: State—6 pounds, 1.9 ounces; Lake Michigan, Kewaunee County, 2001; North American—12 pounds, 9 ounces; Moose and Kenai Rivers, Alaska, 1974

Notes: This Pacific salmon was unintentionally released into Thunder Bay in 1956 and has since spread throughout the Great Lakes. It spends two to three years in the open lake then moves into streams to spawn and die. Often seen along the lakeshore during the odd-year spawning run, less common in even years. Pink Salmon are not often caught by anglers and are not considered great table fare; the flesh deteriorates rapidly and must be quickly put on ice.

107

Description: silver with faint pink or purple tinge; dark back; light-colored tail; small mouth; long body but deeper than Rainbow Smelt

Similar Species: Lake Whitefish (pg. 110); Mooneye (pg. 78), Rainbow Smelt (pg. 116)

Cisco	**Lake Whitefish**
jaws equal length or slight underbite	snout protrudes beyond lower jaw

Cisco	**Mooneye**
adipose fin	lacks adipose fin

Cisco	**Rainbow Smelt**
deep body (also inconspicuous teeth)	slim profile (also prominent teeth)

CISCO
Coregonus artedi

Other Names: shallow water, common or Great Lakes cisco, lake herring, tullibee

Habitat: shoal waters of the Great Lakes and nutrient-poor inland lakes with oxygen-rich depths that remain cool during the summer

Range: northeastern U.S., Great Lakes and Canada; in Wisconsin, shallow coastal waters of lakes Superior and Michigan, and deep, nutrient-poor inland lakes in the Mississippi, Superior and Michigan drainages

Food: plankton, small crustaceans, aquatic insects

Reproduction: spawns in November and December when water temperatures reach the lower 30s; eggs are deposited over clean bottoms, usually in 3 to 8 feet of water

Average Size: 10 to 12 inches, 12 ounces

Records: State—4 pounds, 10.5 ounces; Big Green Lake, Green Lake County, 1969; North American—7 pounds, 4 ounces; Cedar Lake, Manitoba, 1986

Notes: Ciscoes were once the most productive commercial fish in the Great Lakes. They are still common in Superior but threatened in Lake Michigan. Many "smoked whitefish" sold today are really ciscoes. The inland forms of ciscoes are known as tullibees and vary greatly in size from one lake to another. Ciscoes can be caught through the ice in winter, or by fly fishermen in the summer.

Description: silver with dark brown to olive back and tail; snout protrudes past lower jaw; mouth is small, with two small flaps between the openings of each nostril

Similar Species: Cisco (pg. 108), Mooneye (pg. 78), Rainbow Smelt (pg. 116)

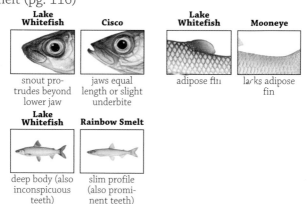

Lake Whitefish	Cisco	Lake Whitefish	Mooneye
snout protrudes beyond lower jaw	jaws equal length or slight underbite	adipose fin	lacks adipose fin

Lake Whitefish	Rainbow Smelt
deep body (also inconspicuous teeth)	slim profile (also prominent teeth)

LAKE WHITEFISH
Coregonus clupeaformis

Other Names: eastern, common or Great Lakes whitefish, gizzard fish, Sault whitefish

Habitat: large, deep, clean inland lakes with cool, oxygen-rich depths during the summer; shallow areas of the Great Lakes

Range: from the Great Lakes north across North America; in Wisconsin, mostly in the north and eastern parts of the state, and lakes Michigan and Superior; rarely in the Mississippi drainage

Food: zooplankton, insects, small fish

Reproduction: spawns on shallow gravel bars in late fall when water temperatures reach the low 30s; occasionally ascends streams to spawn

Average Size: 18 inches, 3 to 5 pounds

Records: State—11 pounds, 11 ounces; Lake Superior, Iron County, 1977; North American—15 pounds, 6 ounces; Clear Lake, Ontario, 1983

Notes: Lake Whitefish are the largest whitefish in North America. It was once common in all Great Lakes but is now abundant only in Lake Superior and northern Lake Michigan. Primarily a lake resident, the Lake Whitefish has been taken from a few streams, including the Brule and Menominee rivers. A fine food fish, it was once as important as Lake Trout in Wisconsin's commercial fishing industry. Anglers most commonly fish for whitefish through the ice in winter.

Description: blotchy brown coloration; large mouth; eyes set almost on top of the broad head; large, winglike pectoral fins; lacks scales

Similar Species: Round Goby

Mottled Sculpin	Round Goby
lacks scales	scales on body

MOTTLED SCULPIN
Cottus bairdii

Other Names: common sculpin, muddler or gudgeon

Habitat: cool, hard-water streams and clear lakes; favors areas with rocks or vegetation

Range: eastern U.S. through Canada to Hudson Bay and the Rocky Mountains; streams and some lakes in all three Wisconsin drainage basins, and lakes Superior and Michigan

Food: aquatic invertebrates, fish eggs, small fish

Reproduction: spawns in April and May at water temperatures of 63 to 74 degrees; male fans out cavity beneath a rock, ledge or log and attracts females through courtship displays such as head nodding, head shaking and gill cover raising; spawning fish turn upside down and deposit eggs on underside of nest cover; male guards and cleans nest after spawning

Average Size: 4 to 5 inches

Records: none

Notes: The most common sculpin in Wisconsin, it can be found in many cool streams (averaging 68 degrees) and in some northern lakes with clear water and rocky bottoms. Though scary looking, it is perfectly harmless and a food source for a variety of predators, which it avoids by modifying its body color to blend in with the surroundings. The closely related sculpins of Lake Superior are important forage fish for Lake Trout. The Slimy Sculpin inhabits shallow areas and tributary streams, while the Deepwater and Spoonhead Sculpin occupy Superior's icy depths.

Description: long, thin body; sides bright silver with conspicuous black stripe; upturned mouth; two dorsal fins

Similar Species: Common Shiner (pg. 74), Rainbow Smelt (pg. 116)

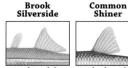

Brook Silverside **Common Shiner** **Rainbow Smelt**

two dorsal fins single dorsal fin single dorsal fin

BROOK SILVERSIDE
Labidesthes sicculus

Other Names: northern or brook silverside, skipjack, friar

Habitat: surface of clear lakes and large streams

Range: southeastern U.S. to the Great Lakes; common in the clear lakes and larger streams in south-central Wisconsin, uncommon in the northeast

Food: aquatic and flying insects, spiders

Reproduction: spawns in late spring and early summer; eggs are laid in sticky strings that attach to vegetation; adults die soon after spawning

Average Size: 3 to 4 inches

Records: none

Notes: The Brook Silverside belongs to a large family of fish that is mostly tropical and subtropical, and primarily found in saltwater. It is a flashy fish often seen cruising near the surface in small schools. Its upturned mouth is an adaptation to surface feeding, and it is not uncommon to see a Brook Silverside leap from the water, flying fish style, in pursuit of prey. Because of this tendency to jump, coupled with a lack of hardiness when kept in captivity, it is a poor aquarium fish despite its beauty.

Description: large mouth with prominent teeth; jaw extends to rear margin of the eye; dark green back; violet-blue sides and white belly; deeply forked tail; adipose fin

Similar Species: Cisco (pg. 108), Lake Whitefish (pg. 110); Mooneye (pg. 78), Common Shiner (pg. 74), Brook Silverside (pg. 114)

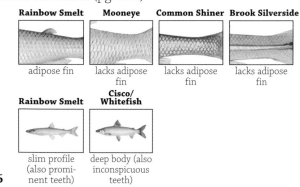

Rainbow Smelt	Mooneye	Common Shiner	Brook Silverside
adipose fin	lacks adipose fin	lacks adipose fin	lacks adipose fin

Rainbow Smelt	Cisco/ Whitefish
slim profile (also prominent teeth)	deep body (also inconspicuous teeth)

RAINBOW SMELT

Osmerus mordax

Other Names: ice or frost fish, lake herring, leefish

Habitat: open oceans and large lakes, tributaries at spawning

Range: Coastal Pacific, Atlantic and Arctic oceans, landlocked lakes in northeast U.S. and southeast Canada; in Wisconsin, Lakes Superior and Michigan, and a few lakes in Forest and Bayfield counties

Food: crustaceans, insect larvae, small fish

Reproduction: spawning takes place in May, at night, in the first mile of tributary streams

Average Size: 8 to 10 inches

Records: none

Notes: Smelt are marine fish that enter freshwater to spawn. In 1912 they were introduced into some Michigan lakes to support salmon stocks. Smelt soon escaped into Lake Michigan and made it to Lake Superior in 1930. The small fish was soon making spectacular spawning runs, and smelt fishing became a spring ritual. The smelt carnival reached its peak during the late 1930s when Oconto and Marinette, Wisconsin attracted up to 30,000 visitors. The Great Lakes smelt population crashed in the 1980s and has not fully recovered. Where it has been introduced in inland lakes, the Rainbow Smelt is excellent forage for large predators such as Walleyes, but some biologists link it to eventual declines in predator populations, due to predation on young game fish or competition for food.

117

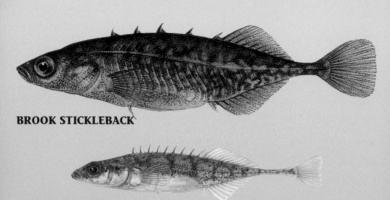

BROOK STICKLEBACK

NINESPINE STICKLEBACK

Description: both Brook and Ninespine Sticklebacks are brown with torpedo-shaped body and very narrow caudal peduncle (area just before the tail); front portion of dorsal fin has short, separated spines; pelvic fins are abdominal and reduced to a single spine; small, sharp teeth

Similar Species: Brook Stickleback, Ninespine Stickleback

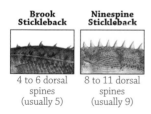

Brook Stickleback	Ninespine Stickleback
4 to 6 dorsal spines (usually 5)	8 to 11 dorsal spines (usually 9)

BROOK STICKLEBACK

Gasterosteidae

Culaea inconstans

Other Names: common or many-spined-stickleback, spiny minnow

Habitat: shallows of cool streams and lakes

Range: Kansas through the northern U.S. and Canada; common in cool streams in most of Wisconsin

Food: feeds on small aquatic animals, occasionally algae

Reproduction: in water temperatures from 50 to 68 degrees, male builds a golf ball-sized, globular nest of sticks, algae and other plant matter on submerged vegetation; females deposit eggs and depart, often plowing a hole in the side of the nest in the process; the male repairs any damage and viciously guards the eggs until hatching; an ambitious male may build a second, larger nest and transfer the eggs there by mouth

Average Size: 2 to 4 inches

Records: none

Notes: Most members of the stickleback family are marine fish but some are equally at home in fresh or saltwater. Anglers are most likely to encounter a Brook Stickleback in the bait pail mixed in with small fatheads or "crappie minnows." Though often discarded in disgust, they do work well as bait. These pugnacious little predators also make fun aquarium fish, and will readily build and defend nests in captivity. Another stickleback, the Ninespine, is restricted to lakes Superior and Michigan.

Description: slate gray to brown sides, white belly; bony plates on skin; tail lacks plates and is shark-like, with upper lobe longer than lower; blunt snout with four barbels; spiracles (openings between eye and corner of gill)

Similar Species: Shovelnose Sturgeon (pg. 122)

Lake Sturgeon

Shovelnose Sturgeon

spiracle between
eye and gill

lacks spiracles

LAKE STURGEON
Acipenser fulvescens

Acipenseridae

Other Names: rock sturgeon, smoothback

Habitat: quiet waters of large rivers and lakes

Range: Hudson Bay, Great Lakes, Mississippi and Missouri drainages southeast to Alabama; in Wisconsin, once common in large rivers and lakes throughout the state, now rare to uncommon in most areas

Food: snails, clams, crayfish, aquatic insects

Reproduction: spawns April through June in lake shallows and tributary streams; a single female may produce up to 1 million eggs

Average Size: 20 to 55 inches, 5 to 40 pounds

Records: State—170 pounds, 10 ounces; Yellow Lake, Burnett County, 1979 (not registered as a North American record); North American—168 pounds; Nattawasaga Lake, Ontario, 1982

Notes: The Lake Sturgeon is the largest fish in Wisconsin, historically reaching weights of more than 200 hundred pounds. Before the 1870s it was considered a nuisance fish, and many wagonloads were left to rot on shorelines. These slow-growing fish don't reproduce until they are over 20 years old, and may live to be 75 or more. There is a very limited season and bag limit in Wisconsin.

Description: coppery, dark tan or light brown back and sides; light belly; long, flat snout; shovel-shaped head; bony plates instead of scales; shark-like tail with upper lobe ending in a long filament

Similar Species: Lake Sturgeon (pg. 120)

Shovelnose Sturgeon	Lake Sturgeon
lacks spiracles	spiracle between eye and gill

SHOVELNOSE STURGEON

Scaphirhynchus platorynchus

Other Names: hackleback, sand sturgeon, switchtail

Habitat: open, flowing channels of rivers and large streams, typically with sand or gravel bottom

Range: Hudson Bay south through central U.S., west to New Mexico and east to Kentucky; in Wisconsin, the Mississippi River drainage and some of its large tributaries

Food: clams, snails, crayfish, aquatic insects

Reproduction: spawns in May and June at water temperatures of 65-71 degrees; adults migrate upriver or into small tributaries to spawn over gravel or rocks in swift current; when necessary, will also spawn below dams

Average Size: 24 inches, 3 pounds

Records: State—7 pounds, 5.4 ounces; Mississippi River, Vernon County, 1998; North American—8 pounds, 5 ounces; Rock River, Illinois, 2003

Notes: The Shovelnose Sturgeon is the smallest sturgeon in North America. The prehistoric-looking family to which it belongs has cartilage instead of bones and hard plates in place of scales. Like the Lake Sturgeon, it suctions food off the bottom. The Shovelnose Sturgeon is netted commercially in Wisconsin for both meat and caviar. The meat is oily and is best when smoked or baked.

Description: olive brown to bronze back; sides dull olive fading to white belly; blunt snout; rounded head; long dorsal fin; upper lip even with lower margin of eye

Similar Species: Common Carp (pg. 66), Black Buffalo (pg. 126), Smallmouth Buffalo (pg. 128)

Bigmouth Buffalo

upper lip level with lower edge of eye

Black Buffalo

upper lip well below eye

Smallmouth Buffalo

upper lip well below eye

Bigmouth Buffalo

forward-facing mouth, lacks barbels

Common Carp

down-turned mouth with barbels

BIGMOUTH BUFFALO
Ictiobus cyprinellus

Other Names: baldpate, blue router, mongrel, round buffalo

Habitat: soft-bottomed shallows of large lakes, sloughs and oxbows; slow-flowing streams and rivers

Range: Saskatchewan to Lake Erie south through Mississippi River drainage to the Gulf of Mexico; in Wisconsin, all of the Mississippi River drainage, but most widely distributed in the Rock River drainage in the south

Food: small mollusks, insect larvae, zooplankton

Reproduction: makes spectacular spawning runs in clear, shallow water of flooded fields and marshes during April and May when water temperatures reach the low 60s

Average Size: 18 to 20 inches, 10 to 12 pounds

Records: State—73 pounds, 2 ounces, Lake Koshkonong, Jefferson County, 2004; North American—73 pounds, 1 ounce, Lake Koshkonong, Wisconsin, 2004

Notes: This large, schooling fish is a filter feeder. It is commercially harvested in the lower Mississippi River but not often taken on hook and line. One exception to this was in 2004, when the world record was caught in Wisconsin. Bigmouth Buffalo can tolerate low oxygen levels, high water temperatures and some turbidity but prefer clean, clear water. This big, strong fighter is good to eat and would be a world-class sport fish if it would more readily take a hook.

Description: slate-green to dark gray back; sides have a blue-bronze sheen; deep-bodied with a sloping back supporting a long dorsal fin; upper lip well below eye

Similar Species: Common Carp (pg. 66), Bigmouth Buffalo (pg. 124), Smallmouth Buffalo (pg. 128)

Black Buffalo	Bigmouth Buffalo	Smallmouth Buffalo
upper lip well below eye	upper lip level with lower edge of eye	upper lip well below eye

Black Buffalo	Common Carp
mouth lacks barbels	barbels below mouth

126

BLACK BUFFALO

Ictiobus niger

Other Names: buoy tender, current or deep-water buffalo

Habitat: deep, fast water of large streams; deep sloughs, backwaters and impoundments

Range: lower Great Lakes and Mississippi drainages west to South Dakota, south to New Mexico and Louisiana; in Wisconsin, the Mississippi River, lower Wisconsin and Pecatonica rivers

Food: aquatic insects, crustaceans, algae

Reproduction: spawning takes place in April and May when fish move up tributaries to lay eggs in flooded sloughs and marshes

Average Size: 15 to 20 inches, 10 to 12 pounds

Records: State—no record; North American—63 pounds, 6 ounces; Mississippi River, Iowa, 1999

Notes: The Black Buffalo is a southern species that inhabits the deep, strong currents of large rivers. It is rare to uncommon in Wisconsin, and on the threatened species list. Not often caught by anglers, the Black Buffalo occasionally makes up the larger fish in a commercial catch. Any Black Buffalo caught on hook and line should be reported to the DNR.

Description: slate green back with bronze sides; large, dark eye; deep, laterally compressed body; rounded head; blunt snout; small, downturned mouth with thick lips

Similar Species: Common Carp, (pg. 66), Bigmouth Buffalo (pg. 124), Black Buffalo (pg. 126)

Smallmouth Buffalo
upper lip well below eye

Bigmouth Buffalo
upper lip level with eye

Smallmouth Buffalo
mouth lacks barbels

Common Carp
barbels below mouth

Smallmouth Buffalo
back steeply arched with pronounced hump

Black Buffalo
rounded back without hump

SMALLMOUTH BUFFALO

Ictiobus bubalus

Other Names: razorback, highback or humpback buffalo, thick-lipped buffalo

Habitat: moderate to swift currents in the deep, clean water of larger streams and lakes

Range: the Missouri, Mississippi and Ohio River drainages south to the Gulf and west into New Mexico; in Wisconsin, only found in the Mississippi River drainage

Food: insect larvae, small crustaceans

Reproduction: spawns in flooded fields and marshes in early summer when water temperatures reach the low 60s

Average Size: 10 to 15 inches, 3 to 5 pounds

Records: State—20 pounds; Milwaukee River, Washington County, 1999—88 pounds, Lake Wylie, North Carolina, 1993

Notes: This smaller cousin of the Bigmouth Buffalo is uncommon in most streams but may be the predominant buffalo in others. The Smallmouth Buffalo requires clean, clear water and is now on the increase with the cleanup of the Mississippi River in the past twenty years. It rarely takes a hook, so is not a significant sport fish—but is an important food fish, commercially harvested in the St. Croix and Mississippi rivers.

Description: bright silver, often with yellow tinge; fins clear; deep body with round, blunt head; leading rays of dorsal fin extend into a large, arching "quill"

Similar Species: Common Carp (pg. 66), Smallmouth Buffalo, (pg. 128)

Quillback	Common Carp	Quillback	Smallmouth Buffalo
mouth lacks barbels	barbels below mouth	longest dorsal ray similar to base	longest dorsal ray much shorter than base

QUILLBACK
Carpiodes cyprinus

Other Names: silver carp, carpsucker, lake quillback

Habitat: slow-flowing streams and rivers; backwaters and lakes, particularly areas with soft bottoms

Range: south-central Canada through the Great Lakes to the eastern U.S., south through the Mississippi drainage to the Gulf; Mississippi and Lake Michigan drainages in the southern two-thirds of Wisconsin

Food: insects, plant matter, decaying material on bottom

Reproduction: ascends tributaries from late spring through early summer; spawns over sand, gravel or mud

Average Size: 14 inches, 1 to 3 pounds

Records: State—8 pounds, 7.2 ounces; Fox River, Green Lake County, 2002; North American—8 pounds, 13 ounces; Lake Winnebago, Wisconsin, 2003

Notes: The Quillback is the most common of the three carp-suckers found in Wisconsin. It is a pretty, silver fish that travels in schools and filter feeds in the quiet waters of many Wisconsin lakes and streams. It is reportedly of good flavor, but of little importance to anglers. Quillbacks are a small part of the Mississippi River commercial harvest.

Description: olive brown to brownish back; sides silver to bronze; white belly; bright red tail; blunt nose; sickle-shaped dorsal fin

Similar Species: Longnose Sucker (pg. 134), White Sucker, (pg. 136)

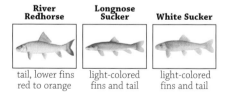

River Redhorse	Longnose Sucker	White Sucker
tail, lower fins red to orange	light-colored fins and tail	light-colored fins and tail

RIVER REDHORSE

Moxostoma carinatum

Other Names: redhorse, sucker

Habitat: clean streams and rivers with sand, gravel or rocky bottom; found in a few clear lakes

Range: Great Lake states to New England south to the Gulf; clear, clean streams and some lakes throughout Wisconsin

Food: insects, crustaceans, mussels, plant debris

Reproduction: spawns from late May to June in small tributary streams; researchers have observed the male building a 4- to 8-foot-diameter nest on gravel shoal, then courting females by darting back and forth across the nest; a second male may join the display and spawning process

Average Size: 12 to 24 inches, 2 to 10 pounds

Records: State—none; North American—8 pounds, 11 ounces; Trent River, Ontario, 1997

Notes: There are six types of redhorse in Wisconsin—the Northern, Silver, Greater, Black, River and Golden—ranging from 2 to 10 pounds. All are "sucker-type fish" similar in appearance. They are clean-water fish, susceptible to increased turbidity and pollutants. They are common in streams but found in only a few lakes. They may look nearly alike but each is a separate species and occupies its own niche in Wisconsin waters. Not of sporting importance but the River Redhorse is a fairly common catch for river anglers fishing angleworms on light split shot or slip-sinker rigs on the bottom. Fights well on light tackle.

133

Description: black, brown to dark olive back; slate to pale brown sides fading to white belly; males develop red band during breeding; long snout protruding beyond upper lip

Similar Species: River Redhorse, (pg. 132), White Sucker (pg. 136)

Longnose Sucker

snout extends well beyond upper lip

White Sucker

snout barely extends past upper lip

Longnose Sucker

fins white to yellowish

River Redhorse

fins red to orange

LONGNOSE SUCKER

Catostomus catostomus

Other Names: sturgeon, red or redside sucker

Habitat: primarily shallow waters of large, cold lakes and streams; sometimes found in deeper water

Range: Siberia across Canada through Great Lakes to the eastern U.S.; Lake Superior and its tributaries; in Wisconsin, Green Bay and Door County waters of the Lake Michigan drainage

Food: small crustaceans, plant material

Reproduction: spawns in April and May, when fish crowd small tributaries

Average Size: 15 to 20 inches, 2 pounds

Records: State—no record; North American—6 pounds, 14 ounces; St. Joseph River, Michigan, 1986

Notes: This northern, cold-water fish is most common in Lake Superior, and was once common in Green Bay but now is on the decline in that area. Longnose Suckers are not often hooked by anglers, but are frequently gathered during the spawning run with nets or spears. They are delicious when smoked and considered by some to surpass the white sucker in flavor.

Description: A cylindrical-shaped fish, 15 to 18 inches long with a rounded head. The snout barely extends beyond the upper lip. The back is olive, brown or black; sides gray to silver with faint dark patches; and the belly is white. The dorsal and tail fin are slate colored; the other fins are tinged orange. Breeding males develop black and purple bands that can fade within minutes when the fish is handled.

Similar Species: Longnose Sucker (pg. 134)

White Sucker

Longnose Sucker

55 to 75 lateral
line scales

90 or more
scales on lateral
line

WHITE SUCKER
Catostomus commersonii

Other Names: common, coarse-scaled or eastern sucker, bay fish, black mullet

Habitat: all permanent waterbodies that can sustain fish

Range: Canada through central and eastern U.S. south to a line from New Mexico to South Carolina; statewide in Wisconsin

Food: insects, crustaceans, plant matter

Reproduction: migrates up tributaries in April and May (often until passage is blocked) to spawn in riffles; in large lakes, spawning may occur along shoreline shallows over gravel or coarse sand bottoms

Average Size: 12 to 18 inches, 1 to 3 pounds

Records: State—6 pounds, 2 ounces; Miller Flowage, Taylor County, 1997, North American—7 pounds, 4 ounces; Big Round Lake, Wisconsin, 1978

Notes: The White Sucker is probably the most common fish in Wisconsin and the most tolerant of all water conditions. It is commercially harvested for animal and human consumption; the flesh is firm and good tasting, often used in fish sticks, soups and chowders. It is also a mainstay in the bait industry. White Suckers are not the great consumers of trout eggs they were once thought to be, but may compete with trout fry for food when first hatched. However, the tremendous forage source young suckers provide for game fish more than offsets this competition.

137

Description: dark green back, greenish sides often with dark lateral band; belly white to gray; large, forward-facing mouth; lower jaw extends to rear margin of eye

Similar Species: Smallmouth Bass (pg. 140)

Largemouth Bass

Smallmouth Bass

mouth extends beyond non-red eye

mouth does not extend beyond red eye

LARGEMOUTH BASS

Micropterus salmoides

Other Names: black bass, green bass, green trout, slough bass

Habitat: shallow, fertile, weedy lakes and river backwaters; weedy bays and extensive weedbeds of larger lakes

Range: southern Canada through U.S. into Mexico, widely introduced; common throughout Wisconsin

Food: small fish, frogs, crayfish, insects, leeches

Reproduction: in May and June when water temperatures reach 60 degrees, male builds nest in 2 to 8 feet of water, usually on firm bottom in weedy cover; female deposits 2,000 to 40,000 eggs, which the male fans and guards; male also protects fry until the "brood swarm" disperses

Average Size: 12 to 20 inches, 1 to 5 pounds

Records: State—11 pounds, 3 ounces, Lake Ripley, Jefferson County, 1940; North American—22 pounds, 4 ounces, Montgomery Lake, Georgia, 1932

Notes: Largest member of the sunfish family in Wisconsin. Most popular game fish in the U.S., the largemouth is known for strong fights and high leaps. Though it is not highly regarded as table fare in the North, it is commonly eaten in the South. A carnivore, it will devour any live prey that fits into its mouth. Found in thick weedbeds, shallow woody cover and around docks; often feeds near the surface; not commonly located in water deeper than 20 feet.

Description: back and sides mottled dark green to bronze or pale gold, often with dark vertical bands; white belly; stout body; large, forward-facing mouth; red eye

Similar Species: Largemouth Bass (pg. 138)

Smallmouth Bass

mouth does not extend beyond red eye

Largemouth Bass

mouth extends beyond non-red eye

SMALLMOUTH BASS

Micropterus dolomieu

Other Names: bronzeback, brown or redeye bass, redeye, white or mountain trout

Habitat: clear, swift-flowing streams and rivers; clear lakes with gravel or rocky shorelines

Range: extensively introduced throughout North America; common throughout Wisconsin, most prevalent in the northeast

Food: small fish, crayfish, insects, frogs

Reproduction: in May and June, when water temperature reaches mid- to high 60s, male sweeps out nest in gravel bed, typically in 3 to 10 feet of water; in lakes, nest is often next to a log or boulder; female lays 2,000 to 14,000 eggs; male guards nest and young until fry disperse

Average Size: 12 to 20 inches, 1 to 4 pounds

Records: State—9 pounds, 1 ounce; Indian Lake, Oneida County, 1950; North American—11 pounds, 15 ounces; Dale Hollow Lake, Tennessee, 1955

Notes: Revered by anglers as a world-class game fish, noted for powerful fights and spectacular jumps. The most renowned smallmouth fishing in Wisconsin is around the Door County peninsula in Lake Michigan. Often feeds near the surface and are a favorite with fly fishermen. Though it is often released, its white flesh is superb table fare, ranked by some only behind trout and whitefish.

141

Description: black to dark olive back; silver sides with dark green or black blotches; back slightly more arched—and depression above eye less pronounced—than White Crappie

Similar Species: White Crappie (pg. 144)

Black Crappie	**White Crappie**	**Black Crappie**	**White Crappie**
usually 7 to 8 spines in dorsal fin	usually 5 to 6 spines in dorsal fin	dorsal fin length equal to distance from dorsal to eye	dorsal fin shorter than distance from eye to dorsal

BLACK CRAPPIE

Pomoxis nigromaculatus

Other Names: papermouth, speck, speckled perch

Habitat: quiet, clear water of streams and mid-sized lakes; often associated with weed growth but may roam deep, open basins and flats, particularly during winter

Range: southern Manitoba through the Atlantic and southeastern states, introduced in the West; in Wisconsin, common in all three drainages

Food: small fish, aquatic insects, zooplankton

Reproduction: spawns in shallow weedbeds from May to June when water temperatures reach the high 50s; male sweeps out circular nest, typically on fine gravel or sand; female may produce more than 180,000 eggs; male guards nest and fry until young crappies are feeding on their own

Average Size: 7 to 12 inches, 10 ounces to 1 pound

Records: State—4 pounds, 8 ounces; Gile Flowage, Iron County, 1967; North American—6 pounds; Westwego Canal, Louisiana, 1969

Notes: Pursued by Wisconsin panfish anglers year-round for its sweet-tasting white fillets, it is an aggressive carnivore that will hit everything from waxworms and fatheads to jigging spoons. Not noted as a tremendous fighter, but puts up a good struggle on light tackle. Actively feeds at night. Prefers cleaner water and more vegetation than the White Crappie, and nests in somewhat shallower water.

Description: greenish back; silvery green to white sides with 7 to 9 dark, vertical bars; the only sunfish with six spines in both the dorsal and anal fin

Similar Species: Black Crappie (pg. 142)

White Crappie	**Black Crappie**	**White Crappie**	**Black Crappie**
usually 5 to 6 spines in dorsal fin	usually 7 to 8 spines in dorsal fin	dorsal fin shorter than distance from eye to dorsal	dorsal fin length equal to distance from dorsal to eye

WHITE CRAPPIE
Pomoxis annularis

Centrarchidae

Other Names: silver, pale or ringed crappie, papermouth

Habitat: slightly silty streams and midsize lakes; prefers less vegetation than Black Crappie

Range: North Dakota south and east to Gulf and Atlantic, except peninsular Florida; southern Wisconsin in both the Mississippi and Lake Michigan drainage

Food: aquatic insects, small fish, plankton

Reproduction: spawns on firm sand or gravel bottom in May and June when water temperature approaches 60 degrees; male fans out nest, guards eggs and young after spawning

Average Size: 6 to 12 inches, 8 to 16 ounces

Records: State—3 pounds, 13 ounces; Cranberry Marsh, Monroe County, 2002; North American—5 pounds, 3 ounces; Enid Dam, Mississippi, 1957

Notes: Popular with anglers but less common in Wisconsin than the Black Crappie. Prefers deeper, less weedy, slightly more turbid water. May be increasing in abundance with the increased silting of streams and lakes. Often found in large schools. Actively feeds at night and during the winter. Due to its acceptance of turbid water, there is some indication of a positive relationship between the White Crappie and Common Carp. An excellent fish for the table with white, fine-flavored meat similar to Black Crappie.

Description: round, flat body; spines in dorsal and anal fins; small mouth; dark olive to green on back, blending to silver-gray, copper, orange, purple or brown on sides with 5 to 9 dark, vertical bars that may fade with age; yellow underside and copper breast, which intensifies on spawning males; large, dark gill spot; dark spot on rear margin of dorsal fin

Similar Species: Green Sunfish (pg. 148), Pumpkinseed (pg. 152)

Bluegill	**Green Sunfish**		**Bluegill**	**Pumpkinseed**
small mouth	large mouth		dark gill spot	orange crescent

Bluegill	**Pumpkinseed**
dark spot on dorsal fin	no dark spot

146

BLUEGILL

Centrarchidae

Lepomis macrochirus

Other Names: 'gill, bull, bream, copperbelly

Habitat: medium to large streams and most lakes with weedy bays or shorelines

Range: southern Canada into Mexico; in Wisconsin, common throughout the state

Food: insects, small fish, leeches, snails, zooplankton, algae

Reproduction: spawns from late May to early August; "parental" male excavates nest in gravel or coarse sand, often in shallow weeds, in colony of up to 50 other nests; often, a smaller "cuckholder" male darts into the nest and fertilizes eggs; parental male guards nest until fry disperse

Average Size: 6 to 9 inches, 5 to 10 ounces

Records: State—2 pounds, 9.8 ounces, Green Bay, Brown County, 1995; North American—4 pounds, 12 ounces, Ketona Lake, Alabama, 1950

Notes: A favorite of anglers young and old for its tenacious fight and excellent table quality. Small fish are easy to catch near docks in summer. Larger "bulls" favor deep weedlines much of the year; during the spawn, colonies are targeted and sometimes overfished. Hybridizes with other sunfish. Has acute daytime vision for feeding on small prey items, but sees poorly in low light. This characteristic makes it easy prey for large predators with good nighttime vision.

Description: dark green back; dark olive to bluish sides; yellow or whitish belly; scales flecked with yellow, producing a brassy appearance; dark gill spot has a pale margin

Similar Species: Bluegill (pg. 146)

Green Sunfish   **Bluegill**

large mouth   small mouth

GREEN SUNFISH

Lepomis cyanellus

Centrarchidae

Other Names: green perch, blue-spotted sunfish, sand bass

Habitat: warm, weedy shallow lakes and the backwaters of slow-moving streams

Range: most of the U.S. into Mexico excluding Florida and the Rocky Mountains; most common in southeast Wisconsin

Food: aquatic insects, crustaceans, small fish

Reproduction: beginning in May, male fans out a nest on gravel bottom, often in less than 1 foot of water, near weeds or other cover beneath overhanging limbs; male may grunt to lure female into nest; after spawning, male guards nest and fans eggs; spawns in water temperatures from 60 to 80 degrees and is capable of producing two broods per season

Average Size: 5 inches, less than 8 ounces

Records: State—1 pound, 9 ounces; Wind Lake, Racine County, 1967; North American—2 pounds, 2 ounces; Stockton Lake, Missouri, 1971

Notes: Very common in the southern third of Wisconsin, the Green Sunfish is abundant in some lakes yet absent from others. Easy to catch but not a popular sport fish because it rarely reaches more than 5 to 7 inches in length. Highly prolific, it may overpopulate a lake with stunted, 3-inch bait robbers and become a major nuisance. Very tolerant of high siltation and low oxygen levels, it thrives in warm, weedy lakes and backwaters. Often hybridizes with Bluegill and Pumpkinseed producing larger, more voracious offspring.

149

Description: bluish green back fading to orange; about 30 orange or red spots on sides of males, brown spots on females; orange pelvic and anal fins; black gill spot has light margin

Similar Species: Bluegill (pg. 146), Green Sunfish (pg. 148), Pumpkinseed (pg. 152)

Orangespotted Sunfish

light margin on gill spot

Bluegill

gill spot lacks light margin

Pumpkinseed

orange or red crescent on gill

Orangespotted Sunfish

hard spines higher than soft rays

Green Sunfish

hard spines shorter than soft rays

ORANGESPOTTED SUNFISH

Lepomis humilis

Other Names: orangespot, dwarf sunfish, pygmy sunfish

Habitat: open to moderately weedy pools with soft bottoms

Range: southern Great Lakes through Mississippi River basin to Gulf States; southern Wisconsin in the Mississippi River drainage as far north as the St. Croix River; lower portions of the Wisconsin River

Food: insects, crustaceans

Reproduction: male builds and guards nest in shallow water when water temperatures reach the mid 60s; colonial nesters

Average Size: 3 to 4 inches, 4 ounces

Records: none

Notes: This brightly colored sunfish is very common in some lakes and although it is often caught, it is too small to be a significant panfish. It does, however, make a colorful aquarium pet. The Orangespotted Sunfish is important as forage species for other game fish and may be important for mosquito larvae control in some areas. It survives well in silty water and tolerates slight pollution, making it well suited for small lakes in agricultural areas.

Description: back brown to olive; sides speckled with orange, yellow, blue and green spots with 7 to 10 vertical bands; chest and belly yellow or orange; black gill spot has light margin with orange or red crescent

Similar Species: Bluegill (pg. 146), Green Sunfish (pg. 148), Orangespotted Sunfish (pg. 150)

Pumpkinseed

orange or red crescent on gill flap

Bluegill

gill spot lacks light margin

Orangespotted Sunfish

light margin on gill spot

Pumpkinseed

long, pointed pectoral fin

Green Sunfish

rounded pectoral fin

PUMPKINSEED

Centrarchidae

Lepomis gibbosus

Other Names: 'seed, punky, yellow or round sunfish, bream

Habitat: weedy ponds, clear lakes, reservoirs and slow-moving streams; prefers slightly cooler water than Bluegill

Range: native to eastern and central North America, widely introduced elsewhere; widely distributed throughout Wisconsin in all three drainage basins, and the shallow protected bays of lakes Superior and Michigan

Food: insects, snails, fish, leeches, small amounts of vegetation

Reproduction: from late May to August starting when water temperatures reach 55 to 63 degrees, male builds nest on gravel bottom among weeds in less than 2 feet of water; nests are located in colonies, often with other sunfish species; female leaves after spawning; male aggressively guards the nest; multiple broods per year common

Average Size: 6 to 8 inches, 6 to 10 ounces

Records: State—1 pound, 2 ounces; Big Round, Polk County, 2003; North American—2 pounds, 4 ounces; North Saluda River, South Carolina, 1997

Notes: A brilliantly-colored sunfish that feeds along edges of deep weedbeds during the day and settles to the bottom at night. Often schools around weeds, docks and sunken logs. Eagerly attacks a variety of small natural and artificial baits including flies. A fine table fish. Hybridizes with other sunfish and stunting is common. Eats insects and small fish; also uses specially adapted teeth to feed on snails.

153

Description: brown to olive green back and sides with dark spots and overall bronze appearance; red eye; thicker, heavier body than other sunfish; large mouth

Similar Species: Bluegill (pg. 146), Green Sunfish (pg. 148), Pumpkinseed (pg. 152), Warmouth (pg. 156)

Rock Bass	**Green Sunfish**	**Pumpkinseed**	**Warmouth**
solid dark gill spot	light margin on gill spot	orange or red crescent on gill flap	dark gill spot with light margin

Rock Bass	**Bluegill**
large mouth extends to eye	small mouth does not extend to eye

ROCK BASS

Ambloplites rupestris

Other Names: redeye, goggle eye, rock sunfish

Habitat: vegetation on firm to rocky bottom in clear-water lakes and medium-size streams

Range: southern Canada through central and eastern U.S. to northern edge of Gulf states; in Wisconsin, common statewide but more abundant in the north

Food: prefers crayfish, but eats aquatic insects and small fish

Reproduction: solitary nester; spawns in spring at water temperatures from high 60s to 70s; male fans out a nest on coarse gravel bottom in weeds less than 3 feet deep; female stays only long enough to deposit eggs; male guards eggs and fry

Average Size: 8 to 10 inches, 8 ounces to 1 pound

Records: State—2 pounds, 15 ounces; Shadow Lake, Waupaca County, 1990; North American—3 pounds, York River, Ontario, 1974

Notes: Though stocky, plentiful, hard-fighting and good tasting, it is not often targeted by anglers. Frequents weeds on rocky or gravel substrate, and is often found in schools that do not stray far from their home territories. Once a school is located, Rock Bass are easy to catch.

155

Description: back and sides greenish gray to brown; lightly mottled with faint vertical bands; stout body; large mouth; red eye; 3 to 5 reddish-brown streaks radiate from eye

Similar Species: Bluegill (pg. 146), Green Sunfish (pg. 148), Pumpkinseed (pg. 152), Rock Bass (pg. 154)

Warmouth	Bluegill	Green Sunfish
jaw extends at least to middle of eye	small mouth does not extend to eye	jaw does not extend to middle of eye

Warmouth	Pumpkinseed	Rock Bass
light margin on gill spot	prominent orange or red crescent on gill spot	dark gill spot lacks light margin

WARMOUTH

Lepomis gulosus

Other Names: goggle-eye, wide-mouth sunfish, stumpknocker, weed bass

Habitat: heavy weeds in turbid (cloudy) lakes, reservoirs and slow-moving streams

Range: southern U.S. from Texas to Florida north to the southern Great Lakes region; southern Wisconsin in both the Mississippi and Lake Michigan drainages

Food: small fish, insects, snails, crustaceans

Reproduction: not a colonial nester like other sunfish; male fans out solitary bed in dense, shallow weeds when water temperatures reach the low 70s; nest is located by a rock, stump or weed clump; male guards eggs after spawning

Average Size: 11 inches, 8 to 12 ounces

Records: State—1 pound, 1 ounce; Eagle Lake, Racine County, 2001; North American—2 pounds, 7 ounces; Yellow River, Florida, 1985

Notes: This secretive sunfish is rare to uncommon in Wisconsin. It is a solitary, sight-feeding fish that, when not hiding in dense vegetation, is often found around rocks and submerged stumps. Prefers turbid water over mud bottoms, and seems to be expanding its range with the increased siltation of lakes and streams in southern Wisconsin.

Description: bright silver; 6 to 8 distinct, uninterrupted black stripes on each side; front hard-spined portion of dorsal fin separated from soft-rayed rear section; lower jaw protrudes beyond snout

Similar Species: Yellow Bass (pg. 160)

White Bass	**Yellow Bass**	**White Bass**	**Yellow Bass**
lower jaw protrudes beyond snout	lower jaw even with snout	stripes continuous	stripes broken above anal fin

WHITE BASS
Morone chrysops

Moronidae

Other Names: silver bass, streaker, lake bass, sand bass

Habitat: large lakes, rivers and impoundments with relatively clear water

Range: Great Lakes region to the eastern seaboard, through the southeast to the Gulf, west to Texas; in Wisconsin, common in the large lakes and rivers in the southern half of the state, and in Green Bay and its large tributaries

Food: small fish

Reproduction: spawns in late spring to early summer at water temperatures of 55 to 79 degrees, in open water over gravel beds or rubble 6 to 10 feet deep; a single female may produce more than 500,000 eggs

Average Size: 18 inches, 8 ounces to 2 pounds

Records: State—4 pounds, 6 ounces; Okauchee Lake, Waukesha County, 2004; North American—6 pounds, 7 ounces; Saginaw Bay, Michigan, 1989

Notes: Both the White and Yellow Bass are native to Wisconsin, where they are considered panfish and highly regarded by anglers. White Bass travel in large "packs" near the surface and can often be spotted by watching for seagulls feeding over the schools. The Wolf River is renowned for the large number of anglers that gather to enjoy the spectacular spawning runs.

Description: silvery yellow to brassy sides with yellowish white belly; 6 or 7 black stripes broken above anal fin; forked tail; two sections of dorsal connected by membrane

Similar Species: White Bass (pg. 158)

Yellow Bass	White Bass	Yellow Bass	White Bass
lower jaw even with snout	jaw protrudes beyond snout	stripes broken above anal fin	stripes continuous

YELLOW BASS
Morone mississippiensis

Other Names: brassy or gold bass, barfish

Habitat: open water over shallow gravel bars

Range: Mississippi River drainage south to the Gulf of Mexico; in Wisconsin, the Mississippi River and backwaters, and the Rock River basin

Food: small fish, insects, crustaceans

Reproduction: spawns in late spring over gravel bars in the mouths of tributary streams

Average Size: 8 to 12 inches, 8 ounces to 1 pound

Records: State—2 pounds, 2 ounces, Lake Montana, Dane County, 1972; North American—2 pounds, 8 ounces, Tennessee River, Alabama, 2000

Notes: A close cousin to the White Bass, this is a southern species that is not very common in Wisconsin. Attempts to extend the Yellow Bass's range beyond the Mississippi basin have been unsuccessful. Its schooling and feeding habits are similar to those of the White Bass but it tends to stay in the middle of the water column or near the bottom. The Yellow Bass is a very popular panfish farther south, where its flaky, white flesh is considered superior to that of White Bass.

Description: olive to blackish green back, fading to silver-green on the sides; no black stripes on the sides of adult fish; two dorsal fins touch but are separated

Similar Species: White Bass (pg. 158), Yellow Bass (pg. 160)

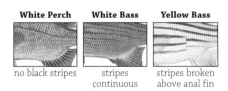

White Perch

no black stripes

White Bass

stripes continuous

Yellow Bass

stripes broken above anal fin

WHITE PERCH

Morone americana

Other Names: narrow-mouth bass, silver or sea perch

Habitat: brackish water in coastal areas, coastal areas of the Great Lakes

Range: invading the Mississippi River drainage south to the Gulf of Mexico; in Wisconsin, Duluth Harbor in Lake Superior, Green Bay and Fox River in Lake Michigan

Food: fish eggs in spring and early summer; minnows, insects and crustaceans

Reproduction: spawning takes place late spring over gravel bars of tributary streams

Average Size: 6 to 8 inches, 1 pound or less

Records: State—1 pound, 8 ounces; Sturgeon Bay, Door County, 2002; North American—4 pounds, 12 ounces; Messalonskee Lake, Maine, 1949

Notes: The White Perch is a coastal Atlantic species that entered the Great Lakes in the 1950s. When available, fish eggs make up 100 percent of its diet in the spring, and it has been linked to Walleye declines in some Canadian waters. If you catch a White Perch anywhere other than in the Duluth Harbor or the Green Bay area, report it to the DNR. Every attempt should be made to contain this invasive species.

Description: overall silvery, almost transparent appearance; mottled brown, tan or greenish with dark spots on sides; adipose fin; single dorsal fin with two spines and 10 to 11 rays

Similar Species: Yellow Perch (pg. 88); Walleye (pg. 86)

Trout-perch	Yellow Perch	Walleye
adipose fin	lacks adipose fin	lacks adipose fin

TROUT-PERCH

Percopsis omiscomaycus

Percopsidae

Other Names: grounder, sand minnow

Habitat: prefers clear to slightly turbid (cloudy) water over sand or gravel; avoids soft-bottomed shallows

Range: east-central U.S. through Canada to Alaska; in Wisconsin, found in all of the larger streams and some large lakes; also present in the intermediate depths of lakes Superior and Michigan

Food: insects, copepods, small fish

Reproduction: spawns from May to August over sand bars and rocks in lakes, or in tributary streams on gravel or sand; two or three males cluster around female, which releases 200 to 700 eggs; fertilized eggs sink to bottom and receive no parental care

Average Size: 3 to 5 inches

Records: none

Notes: A deep-water fish that is seldom seen by humans unless it washes up on the beach, when it is often mistaken for a young Walleye. Has a nocturnal migration pattern and on some nights, large numbers move into the shallows to feed. It is an important forage species for game fish such as Northern Pike and Walleye, and would be a good baitfish, but seining is only productive in the shallows at night.

GLOSSARY

adipose fin a small, fleshy fin without rays, located on the midline of the fish's back between the dorsal fin and the tail

air bladder a balloon-like organ located in the gut area of a fish, used to control buoyancy—and in the respiration of some species such as gar; also called "swim bladder" or "gas bladder"

alevin a newly hatched fish that still has its yolk sac

anadromous a fish that hatches in freshwater, migrates to the ocean, then re-enters streams or rivers to spawn

anal fin a single fin located on the bottom of the fish near the tail

anterior toward the front of a fish, opposite of posterior

bands horizontal marks running lengthwise along the side of a fish

barbel thread-like sensory structures on a fish's head often near the mouth, commonly called "whiskers;" used for taste or smell

bars vertical markings on the side of a fish

benthic organisms living in or on the bottom

brood swarm a large group of young fish such as bullheads

carnivore a fish that feeds on other fish or animals

catadromous a fish that lives in freshwater and migrates into salt-water to spawn, such as the American Eel

caudal fin tail fin

caudal peduncle the portion of the fish's body located between the anal fin and the beginning of the tail

coldwater referring to a species or environment; in fish, often a species of trout or salmon found in water that rarely exceeds 70 degrees; also used to describe a lake or river

copepod a small (less than 2 mm) crustacean that is part of the zooplankton community

crustacean a crayfish, water flea, crab or other animal belonging to group of mostly aquatic species that have paired antennae, jointed legs and an exterior skeleton; common food for many fish

dorsal relating to the top of the fish, on or near the back; opposite of the ventral, or lower, part of the fish

dorsal fin the fin or fins located along the top of a fish's back

eddy a circular water current, often created by an obstruction

epilimnion the warm, oxygen-rich upper layer of water in a thermally stratified lake

exotic a foreign species, not native to a watershed

fingerling a juvenile fish, generally 1 to 10 inches in length, in its first year of life

fork length the overall length of a fish from the mouth to the deepest part of the tail notch

fry recently hatched young fish that have absorbed their yolk sacs

game fish a species regulated by laws for recreational fishing

gills organs used in aquatic respiration

gill cover bone covering the gills, also called opercle or operculum

gill raker a comblike projection from the gill arch

harvest fish that are caught and kept by anglers

hypolimnion bottom layer of water in a thermally stratified lake, usually depleted of oxygen by decaying matter

ichthyologist a scientist who studies fish

invertebrates animals without backbones, such as insects, crayfish, leeches and earthworms

lateral line a series of pored scales along the side of a fish that contain organs used to detect vibrations

littoral zone the part of a lake that is less than 15 feet in depth; this important and often vulnerable area holds the majority of aquatic plants, is a primary area used by young fish, and offers essential spawning habitat for most warmwater fishes

mandible lower jaw

maxillary upper jaw

milt semen of a male fish that fertilizes the female's eggs

mollusk an invertebrate with a smooth, soft body such as a clam

native an indigenous or naturally occurring species

omnivore a fish or animal that eats plants and animal matter

otolith an L-shaped bone found in the inner ear of fish

opercle bone covering the gills, also called gill cover or operculum

panfish small game fish that can be fried whole in a pan

pectoral fins paired fins on the side of the fish behind the gills

pelagic fish species that live in open water, in the food-rich upper layer of water; not associated with the bottom

pelvic fins paired fins below or behind the pectoral fins on the bottom (ventral portion) of the fish

pheromone a chemical scent secreted as a means of communication between members of the same species

piscivore a predatory animal fish that mainly eats other fish

planktivore a fish that feeds on plankton

plankton floating or weakly swimming aquatic plants and animals, including larval fish, that drift with the current; often eaten by fish; individual organisms are called plankters

plankton bloom a marked increase in the amount of plankton due to favorable conditions such as nutrients and light

range the geographic region in which a species is found

ray hard supporting part of the fin; resembles a spine but is jointed

ray soft flexible structures supporting the fin membrane, sometimes branched

redd a nest-like depression made by a male or female fish during the spawn, often refers to nest of trout and salmon species

riprap rock or concrete used to protect a lake shore or river bank from erosion

roe fish eggs

scales small, flat plates covering the outer skin of many fish

Secchi disc a black-and-white circular disk used to measure water clarity; scientists record the average depth at which the disk disappears from sight when lowered into the water

silt small, easily disturbed bottom particles smaller than sand but larger than clay

siltation the accumulation of soil particles

spawning the process of fish reproduction; involves females laying eggs and males fertilizing them to produce young fish

spine stiff, non-jointed structures found along with soft rays

spiracle an opening on the head above and behind the eye

standard length length of the fish from the mouth to the end of the vertebral column

stocking the purposeful, artificial introduction of a fish species

substrate bottom composition of a lake, stream or river

subterminal mouth a mouth below the snout of the fish

swim bladder see air bladder

tailrace area immediately downstream of a dam or power plant

thermocline middle layer of water in a stratified lake, typically oxygen rich, characterized by a sharp drop in water temperature

terminal mouth forward facing

total length the length of the fish from the mouth to the tail compressed to its fullest length

tributary a stream that feeds into another stream, river or lake

turbid cloudy; water clouded by suspended sediments or plant matter that limits visibility and the passage of light

velocity the speed of water flowing in a stream or river

vent the opening at the end of the digestive tract

ventral the underside of the fish

vertebrate an animal with a backbone

warmwater a non-salmonid species of fish that lives in water that routinely exceeds 70 degrees; also used to describe a lake or river according to average summer temperature

yolk the part of an egg containing food for the developing fish

zooplankton the animal component of plankton; tiny animals that float or swim weakly; common food of small fish

PRIMARY REFERENCES

Bailey, R. M. and W. C. Latta, G. R. Smith. 2004
An Atlas of Michigan Fishes
University of Michigan Press

Becker, G. C. 1983
Fishes of Wisconsin
University of Wisconsin Press

Eddy, S. and J. C. Underhill. 1974
Northern Fishes
University of Minnesota Press

Hubbs, C. L. and K. F. Lagler. 1958
Fishes of the Great Lakes Region
University of Michigan Press

McClane, A. J. 1978
Freshwater Fishes of North America
Henery Holt and Company

Phillips, Gary L. and W. D. Schmidt, J. C. Underhill. 1982
Fishes of the Minnesota Region
University of Minnesota Press

INDEX

ABOUT THE AUTHOR

Dave Bosanko was born in Kansas and studied engineering before following his love of nature to degrees in biology and chemistry from Emporia State University. He spent thirty years as staff biologist at two of the University of Minnesota's field stations. Though his training was in mammal physiology, Dave worked on a wide range of research projects ranging from fish, bird and mammal population studies to experiments with biodiversity and prairie restoration. An avid fisherman and naturalist, he has long enjoyed applying the fruits of his extensive field research to patterning fish location and behavior, and observing how these fascinating species interact with one another in the underwater web of life.